I Look at Myself in the Mirror

RICKY CLEMONS

PUBLISHED BY FIDELI PUBLISHING, INC.

ISBN: 978-1-962402-78-1

Published by

Fideli Publishing, Inc.
119 W. Morgan St.
Martinsville, IN 46151
www.FideliPublishing.com

Table of Contents

I Look at Myself in the Mirror

I look at myself in the mirror and I see God's love upon me, who wouldn't know what love is without loving God.

I look at myself in the mirror and I see God's mercy upon me, who is alive today because of God's mercy.

I look at myself in the mirror and I see God's grace upon me, who is in my right mind today because of God's grace.

I look at myself in the mirror and I see God's forgiveness upon me, who knows what it means to forgive myself and others because of God's forgiveness.

I look at myself in the mirror and I see God's long-suffering upon me, who must suffer in denying self and picking up my cross to follow Jesus because of God's long-suffering.

I look at myself in the mirror and I see God's goodness upon me, who is a Christian today because of God's goodness.

I look at myself in the mirror and I see God's healing upon me, who is spiritually healed by the truth of God's holy word because of God's healing power.

I look at myself in the mirror and I see God's protection upon me in my house and wherever I go and come back home safely because of God's protection.

I look at myself in the mirror and I see God's peace upon me, who lives in a troublesome world with a peace of mind because of God's peace.

I look at myself in the mirror and I see God's Holy Spirit upon me, who can love even my enemies and hope that they will believe in Jesus Christ and be saved before it's too late.

I look at myself in the mirror and I see God's salvation upon me, who loves to pray to Jesus and live for Jesus because I love Jesus who gave up His life on the cross to save me from my sins.

I look at myself in the mirror and I see the devil who doesn't want me to see that it's God who is so good to me all the time.

I look at myself in the mirror and I see the devil who doesn't want me to see that it's God who brought me this far in my life because the devil wants me to look at myself in the mirror and believe that I brought myself this far in my life.

I see God with me when I look at myself in the mirror, and I truly know that I am saved in God's Son, Jesus Christ.

I look at myself in the mirror and I see God's strength upon me to keep me mentally, emotionally, physically and spiritually strong in my difficult experiences in life.

I look at myself in the mirror and I see God is with me, and I know that the devil can't deceive me into believing that God is not for me, even though my enemies are against me.

When I look at myself in the mirror, the devil wants me to see only me giving myself the glory and praise for what God is doing for me in my life.

When I look at myself in the mirror, the devil wants me to see only me being caught up in myself, who God kept safe in my mother's womb.

Today, I can look at myself in the mirror and I see that God has given me a second chance to love Him and keep His Commandments; that is God's character.

Today, I can look at myself in the mirror and I see that God didn't leave me all alone when I was living in darkness that would have killed me if God had allowed it.

Today, I can look at myself in the mirror and I see that God is with me, because God has opened my spiritual blind eyes to look into His mirror of Commandments that have no spots or stains on them, when man-made mirrors can get spots and stains on them and not let me see myself clearly.

I look at myself in the mirror and I see no good thing in me without Jesus Christ being in my heart to help me to be good to myself and my neighbors.

I look at myself in the mirror and I see a lost soul if I don't confess and repent of my sins unto the Lord.

If I hold onto even one sin and don't confess and repent of that sin unto Jesus, I will be lost.

Our Shadow Will See Us

Our shadow will see us as a Christian or a hypocrite.

We can be dishonest to our shadow but it will not be dishonest to us and will do whatever we do.

Our shadow will see us as good or evil.

We can be untrustworthy to our shadow, even though we can trust our shadow wherever we go.

Our shadow will see us do right or do wrong.

We can be unstable in our ways but our shadow won't be unstable and won't do something different from what we do, whether we do right or wrong.

Our shadow will see us for who we are.

We can pretend to be who we are not, but our shadow will not pretend with us.

Our shadow moves when we move and will stand still when we stand still.

Our shadow will see us even when we run and hide away from someone.

No matter what we do wrong, our shadow will not run and hide away from someone.

Our shadow is held captive by us and is a slave to whatever we do, even on the spur of the moment.

Our shadow will see us making mistakes, but our shadow won't make any mistakes and will do just what we do.

Our shadow will go wherever we go, and we will see our shadow beside us, below us or in front of us especially at night.

Our shadow will always see us and reflect whatever we do because we can't fool our shadow and our shadow wont' fool us and will always be truthful to us.

Our shadow will stay close, connected to us and we will never think about getting rid of our shadow.

Many people want to get rid of God, who is more connected to us than our shadow for loving Him and doing His will in whatever we do for the Lord.

There were many sick people who believed that they would be healed by even Peter's shadow if he just walked by them.

Our shadow will see us when we are being like Jesus Christ or not like Jesus Christ.

We have a God-given free will to choose in the presence of our shadow that can't choose to do anything different from what we do.

If our shadow could choose to do something different from what we do, then our shadow would scare us to death.

God created us and gave us a shadow to remind us that we are alive to move around here and there as we do God's holy will and not our own will.

Many people are deceitful when their shadow will not deceive them.

Many people are afraid to do what is right when their shadow is never afraid to do what is right by doing whatever they do.

No one's shadow will stand still when they are moving around here and there, but we can stand still when God tells us to move around to spread the gospel of Jesus Christ who created our shadows to move when we move around here and there.

Our shadow will see us not always paying close attention to what we're doing, but our shadow will do whatever we do.

Our shadow can truly show us that Jesus is forevermore true to us than our shadow.

I Believe in Jesus Christ

I believe in Jesus Christ because His goodness to me has led me to confess and repent of my sins.

I believe in Jesus Christ because Jesus has given me more than one chance to live my life unto Him.

I believe in Jesus Christ because Jesus has spared my life from death many times so I could live to see this day.

I believe in Jesus Christ because Jesus didn't give up on me when I had given up on myself.

I believe in Jesus Christ because Jesus is always there for me on my good days and bad days.

I believe in Jesus Christ because Jesus has shown me that He cannot fail me.

I believe in Jesus Christ because Jesus brought me through hardships that no one else could bring me through.

I believe in Jesus Christ because Jesus never turned His back on me even when I had turned my back on Him.

I believe in Jesus Christ because Jesus is always faithful and true to me.

I believe in Jesus Christ because Jesus winked his eye at my ignorance when I didn't know the truth of His holy word.

I believe in Jesus Christ because Jesus never looked down on me with condemnation when I was living in darkness.

I believe in Jesus Christ because Jesus is my best friend every day, and I can talk to Jesus about anything and He will understand.

I believe in Jesus Christ because Jesus is worthy to be praised every day that no one else can do what Jesus can do for me.

I believe in Jesus Christ because Jesus is all-powerful in my life and I live safely in His protection that cannot fail me like luck has failed me many times.

I believe in Jesus Christ because I know that it's Jesus who blesses my mind with the right thoughts so that I can write them down in words about Him to share with others in published books of prose poetry about Him.

I believe in Jesus Christ because Jesus has never forsaken me when I needed Him most.

I believe in Jesus Christ because I know that Jesus has forgiven me of all my past sins.

I believe in Jesus Christ because Jesus didn't turn me down when I decided to give my life to Him after I was all broken down in the devil's lies that I was living.

I believe in Jesus Christ because I know that Jesus has brought me this far in life even though I don't deserve it.

I believe in Jesus Christ because Jesus spiritually operated on my heart and cut out that old sinful me and cleaned me up spiritually to love Him and keep His Commandments in my heart.

I believe in Jesus Christ because Jesus is always on time to answer my prayers, even when I doubt that He hears me.

I believe in Jesus Christ because I know that Jesus loves me the same as He loves everybody else in this world.

I believe in Jesus Christ because Jesus didn't let the devil destroy me when I was living in my sins.

I believe in Jesus Christ because Jesus is the only true One who I can believe in, because no human being on earth can give me eternal life.

I believe in Jesus Christ because I know that only Jesus is worthy to be worshipped above idol gods that can't make a way out of a no way death threat situation.

I believe in Jesus Christ because Jesus has kept me safe from my old sinful self who once tried to take my own life but Jesus stepped in and spared my life so I could live to see this day.

Jesus has the last decision to make that is always right and fair for my life.

I believe in Jesus Christ because Jesus has proven to me that if I was the only sinner living among perfect people who could do everything right, He would give up his life just to save me from my sins to make me perfect and have no sins so I could do everything perfect.

I believe in Jesus Christ because Jesus has opened doors for me that nobody can shut.

I believe in Jesus Christ because Jesus has shown His great mercy on me.

I believe in Jesus Christ because Jesus has helped me to wise up and not do foolish things anymore.

I believe in Jesus Christ because Jesus has shown me that there is nothing too hard for Him to work things out in my life.

I believe in Jesus Christ because Jesus has shown me that He is the healer of ill motives, ill intentions and ill feelings that man-made medicines can't heal.

I believe in Jesus Christ because He so loved me first, when I didn't love myself.

I believe in Jesus Christ because I know that Jesus didn't bring me this far to let me down.

I believe in Jesus Christ because there is no one else who is worthy to believe in above Jesus, who is the Son of God.

I believe in Jesus Christ because Jesus has done things for me and is doing things for me today that no one else can do for me.

I believe in Jesus Christ because I know today, without a doubt, that Jesus kept death from taking me to the grave that I deserved a long time ago and up until this day that Jesus gives the final say-so over life and death that the devil can't override regardless of so many lives that he has already taken to the grave.

I believe in Jesus Christ because I truly know today that Jesus always knows what is best for me and He will save me from being lost in my sins.

No one else will always know what is best for me and will keep me from doing things that will cause me more harm than good.

I believe in Jesus Christ because Jesus has always been truthful with me and has never deceived me, even though at one time I deceived myself and believed that I didn't need Jesus in my life.

Nobody Can Tell Me

Nobody can tell me that God is not good.

Nobody can tell me that God is not kind.

Nobody can tell me that God is not merciful.

Nobody can tell me that God is not miraculous.

Nobody can tell me that God is not a second chance God.

Nobody can tell me that God is not love.

God loves every human being and God loves all animals.

Nobody can tell me that God is not victorious.

The Lord God has blessed me with two little dogs, one is a boy and the other is a girl.

I give them their dog medicine every morning to ease their itching paws and ears.

When I give them their medicine in the form of a pill, I wrap the pill in a turkey slice.

They love the meat so much that they don't spit out the pill.

One morning when I gave my boy dog his medicine, I was a little distracted by the girl dog walking past me.

When I gave the boy dog his medicine, I always use a corn prong holder that I hold tight in my hand.

I use that because my boy dog will bite my fingers trying to get that turkey meat.

That morning when I was distracted, I wasn't holding the corn prong holder tightly enough and when my boy dog leaped up to eat the turkey he pulled the meat and the corn prong holder out of my hand and almost swallowed it.

I was so frightened that he would die if he swallowed that.

It seemed like everything was happening in slow motion and I couldn't do anything to stop him.

I truly know that God intervened right on time and kept my little boy dog from swallowing that corn prong holder that probably would have killed him.

Nobody can tell me that God is not an on-time God who spared my dog from suffering and possible death.

God has spared me from suffering because God didn't allow my dog to die when I was helpless and frozen in my tracks.

God also loves the animals that He created for His pleasure.

God the Father, the Son, and the Holy Spirit showed me a different way to give my little boy dog his medicine after that frightening day.

I realize the Lord had been merciful to me all the times before this when I'd been giving my dogs their medicine.

I truly believe God had been trying to tell me not to use the corn prong holder, but I didn't listen to God.

Thankfully, God is a loving and merciful God who gives us even more than a second chance to get things right before it's too late.

It's Always Good to do Right

It's always good to do right, even if you think no one sees you doing right.

One morning, I went to the Walmart store to buy a loaf of bread.

When I walked up to the self-checkout machine, I used my bank Visa card to pay for the bread.

As I was using my card, some coins came out of the machine— quarters, dimes, nickels and pennies.

The devil tried to tempt me to keep those coins for myself, but the Lord spoke to me to tell the clerk that the machine was giving out coins that didn't belong to me.

I obeyed the voice of the Lord and left those coins in the cup on the machine.

I am so glad I did the right thing and didn't do what the devil wanted me to do.

The devil didn't want me to be like Jesus in the Walmart store, where people could see who is like Jesus and who is not like Jesus.

Jesus Christ is our righteous Lord and our righteous Savior who does everything right from now until eternity.

It's always good to do right, even if no one else is around to see you because God sees everything you and I do.

God will judge us whether we are doing right or wrong.

Is in Our Mind

The battle of good against evil is in our mind every day because the devil tries to tempt us to think evil thoughts, say evil words and do evil deeds.

The battle of good against evil is in our minds every day and God will try to put good thoughts in our minds so that we say good words and do good deeds.

The way we think will be revealed in the words we say.

The way we think will be revealed in the things we do.

The battle of good against evil is in our minds every day and we need to read God's holy word and think on God's Son, Jesus Christ, who is good all the time.

The battle of good against evil is in our minds every day as soon as we wake up out of our sleep in the morning light.

Our mind is a battleground for good and evil to fight it out like being in a world heavyweight boxing match.

Evil wins the battle in the minds of people who don't think on Jesus and don't love Jesus or keep His Commandments.

Good wins the battle in the minds of people who think on Jesus, love Jesus and keep His Commandments every day.

The battle of good against evil is in our minds every second, minute and hour of the day and night, but if we think on Jesus we will have good and righteous thoughts that He will give to us.

The battle of good against evil is in our minds every day that we can think on anything that's not like Jesus to corrupt our thoughts and make us say wrong words and do wrong things.

The battle of good against evil is in our minds every day, so we need to think on God's holy word to fill our minds with thoughts about Jesus Christ, who renews our minds with good thoughts to fight against those evil thoughts every day.

As long as we think on Jesus, our good thoughts will win the battle that will be revealed by our good words and good actions being like Jesus.

The battle of good against evil starts in our minds because in the Bible, Cain had evil thoughts against his brother, Abel, who he was jealous of because Abel gave God a better sacrifice and God accepted it.

Cain's evil thoughts caused him to commit evil actions and he killed his brother Abel.

The battle of good against evil is in our minds, but if our minds stay on thinking about Jesus, evil can't win the battle because our thoughts will be pure, holy and righteous to reveal God's goodness in our good words and good actions.

Even Out of Our Ignorance

God gave us a free will to make choices every day.

When we were little children, we made choices even out of our ignorance of not knowing whether we made good choices or bad choices.

Our free will to choose is the most powerful thing in this world and the devil has no power over our free will choices.

Even out of our ignorance we make choices without knowing what kind of choice we really made, until we see the results of those choices.

There are choices that we are not aware of that we make out of ignorance.

We will reap the choices that we sow even out of our ignorance that God will wink His eye at because we don't know better and make the wrong choices.

God's mercy will surely cover our bad choices made out of our ignorance.

God's mercy will even cover our bad choices that we know are wrong.

You and I can't play around with God's mercy by making bad choices and knowing we are making them, then expecting that God will just continue to overlook these bad choices we knowingly make.

God has given you and me the most powerful thing in this world, and that is our free will to make choices that will affect us from day to day.

Even out of our ignorance we can make choices that cause us to regret them in some kind of way that we may not see for some years.

God is so good to you and me that He allows us to recover from our bad choices made out of our ignorance as well as those we made knowingly.

God allows us to recover from these bad choices by confessing and repenting of our sins and living our lives doing God's holy will.

The Lord God, our Savior Jesus Christ, is more willing to overlook our ignorant choices than the choices we make that we know are bad.

If we know to make the right choices and don't make them, we cause God to be angry at us.

Even out of our ignorance we will make choices that God will judge, as well as judging the choices that we know to make, whether they are good or bad.

Only Jesus made all the right choices.

Jesus was very aware of the choices He made while he lived in this world without sin.

Jesus was never ignorant of any of the choices He made from day to day, until he gave up His life on the cross for our sins.

Because we were born in sin, we will make some choices, even out of our ignorance.

We can make some good choices and some bad choices even out of our ignorance.

Only God can use our choices in ways that we don't understand, but we will see the good results for living our lives unto Jesus Christ with a testimony to amaze the angels in heaven.

Church is What We Make It

Church is what we make it, when we go to church and walk through the church doors.

We can make the church a worshipping Jesus church or we can make the church a social club.

We can make the church a house of prayer or we can make the church a house of gossip.

Church is what we make it every time we go there.

We can make the church united or make the church divided.

We can make the church a peaceful church or make the church a troublesome church.

We can make the church a loving church or make the church a selfish church.

Church is what we make it in our minds and in our hearts beyond the outward church building.

We can make the church a humble church or make the church a proud church.

We can make the church a friendly church or make the church an unfriendly church.

We can make the church an equality church or make the church a discrimination church.

Church is what we make it, inside the church building.

We can make the church all about the bible truth or make the church mixed with truth and lies.

We can make the church a community service church or make the church a locked-up church.

We can make the church a modest apparel church or make the church a fashion show church.

Church is what we make it about — we can make it about Jesus Christ or make it about ourselves.

We can make the church a free will choice church or make the church a controlling church.

We can make the church a holy and righteous church or make the church a worldly church.

We can make the church a living right by example church or make the church a compromising, misleading church.

Church is what we make it when we go to church to assemble ourselves for the purpose of worshipping our Lord and Savior Jesus, who is the head of the church.

Jesus gives us the free will choice to make the church about Him or make the church about deceptive tactics to manipulate those who are weak in their faith in Jesus Christ.

Church is what we make it in our lives inside the church and outside the church where Jesus wants us to be about loving Him and keeping His Commandments.

We can make the church a spreading the good news about Jesus Christ church or make the church a keeping the good news about Jesus to ourselves church.

We can make the church a believing in Jesus church or make the church a living by eyesight church.

We can make the church a vibrant life, whole body church or make the church a spiritually dead church.

There are Some Things We Must Do

We can pray and ask the Lord to work things out for us, but there are some things we must do that the Lord will have us do.

We can pray and ask the Lord to heal our sick dog, but we have to take our sick dog to the veterinarian doctor who the Lord can use to give us the right medicine for our dog to take to get well.

We can pray and ask the Lord to heal us, but we must go to the doctor who the Lord can use to give us the right medicine to take to get well.

We can pray and ask the Lord to help us, but there are things we must do to help ourselves.

There are some things we must do while we pray to the Lord.

We can pray and ask the Lord to help us to eat the right foods, but we must go to the store and buy the right foods to eat.

The Lord has given you and me our part to do beyond what we pray for unto the Lord.

We can pray and ask the Lord to bless us with a job, but we must go and look for a job — the Lord won't look for and find a job for us.

There are some things we must do and not totally rely on our prayers unto the Lord—He will not do every single thing for us.

We can pray and ask the Lord to stop our roof from leaking, but we must do our part and get our rooftop repaired.

We can pray and ask the Lord to keep us in good health, but we must do our part and take good care of ourselves.

There are some miraculous times that we don't have to do anything for the Lord to work things out in our lives because the Lord can protect us from death that can come our way at any time in any place.

There are some miraculous times that prayer alone is all we need for the Lord to show us that we don't have to do anything but believe He will show up on time.

We Don't Have to Make an Appointment with Jesus

We don't have to make an appointment with Jesus to talk to Him about our mental, emotional and spiritual health.

We don't have to make an appointment with Jesus to give us the strength to get through the day.

We don't have to make an appointment with Jesus to heal our broken spirits.

We don't have to make an appointment with Jesus who is always available to talk to us at any given time in any place.

We don't have to make an appointment with Jesus who can give us the strength to keep on going when things all around us are so troublesome.

We don't have to make an appointment with Jesus who can heal our physical, emotional, mental and spiritual wounds so we truly know that He is the Doctor of doctors who will never make the wrong diagnosis.

We don't have to make an appointment with Jesus to give us whatever we need in our lives from day to day.

Jesus is available to us twenty-four hours around the clock because His office is always open for us to see Him who can solve all of our problems.

We don't have to make an appointment with Jesus for a job interview, because Jesus will come to us with work for us to do for Him.

He will never put pressure on us that we can't handle and He will never overwork us while we're building up His church.

Jesus Has to Fix Us

Jesus has to fix us every day from the brokenness of our sins.

Jesus has to fix us every day from the brokenness of our thoughts.

Jesus has to fix us every day from the brokenness of our words.

Jesus has to fix us every day from the brokenness of our intentions.

Jesus has to fix us every day from the brokenness of our minds.

Jesus has to fix us every day from the brokenness of our hearts.

Jesus has to fix us every day from the brokenness of our actions.

Jesus has to fix us every day from the brokenness of our lives.

We need Jesus to fix us every day from the brokenness of our selfish ways.

Jesus has to fix us every day from the brokenness of our eyes that can see to look towards the things in this world and not look towards Jesus.

Jesus has to fix us every day from the brokenness of our ears that can hear the politics and troubles of this world and not hear the holy word of God for us to have faith in Jesus.

Jesus has to fix us every day from the brokenness of our hands that can pick up and hold things that are temporary and not pick up and open the bible to read about eternal things that Jesus is preparing for us.

Jesus has to fix us every day from the brokenness of our feet that can walk into uncertain places and not walk into the household of faith that can be certain to give us a spiritual walk with Jesus, regardless of who walks away from Jesus in the household of faith.

Jesus has to fix us every day from the brokenness of our self-righteousness that can have some wrong-doings to make us to not be like Jesus, whose righteousness makes us right in God's eyesight not seeing our sins that Jesus forgives us for when we confess and repent.

Jesus has to fix us every day that we are struggling with some kind of brokenness in our lives.

Is Only a Temporary Heaven

This world is heaven to a lot of people who are laying up their treasures in this world.

This world is only a temporary heaven and will one day pass away.

This world is heaven to a lot of people who are rich with money and material things that rich people can't take with them to the grave.

This world is only a temporary heaven that won't always last.

This world is heaven to a lot of people who put their trust in this world and not in God.

This world is heaven to a lot of people who put their trust in the government.

This world is heaven to a lot of people who put their trust in their jobs.

This world is heaven to a lot of people who live by the things that they see in this world.

This world is only a temporary heaven that will be like the Titanic ship that sank.

This world is heaven to a lot of people who are caught up in themselves and believe that everything revolves around them.

This world is heaven to a lot of people who are greedy and want to get rich and famous.

This world is heaven to a lot of people who are educated and proud, looking down on those who are feeble-minded.

This world is only a temporary heaven for those who the devil has greatly deceived.

The real, true heaven is where Jesus Christ will one day take us to if we are saved in Him.

There will be eternal life and everlasting love in that real, true heaven.

This world is heaven to a lot of people who live in pleasure and won't give any of their time to God.

This world is heaven to a lot of people who enjoy living in the darkness of their sins and believe that there is no God to love and obey.

This world is a temporary heaven on its way to hell and will take us to hell with it if we don't obey the Holy Spirit's call to repent and live for Jesus Christ.

A Husband and Wife

A husband and wife who pray together is a powerful couple for Jesus to answer their prayers.

A husband and wife who study their bible together is a powerful couple to help each other live right by the bible.

A husband and wife who love Jesus is a powerful couple to keep Jesus' Commandments together.

A husband and wife who keep Jesus first in their marriage is a powerful couple for their children to see that they can't get between them and Jesus.

A husband and wife who go to church together is a powerful couple to set the right example for everyone in the church.

A husband and wife who witness for Jesus together is a powerful couple to change people's lives for the better.

A husband and wife who support each other in their ministry is a powerful couple in the church that Jesus is the head of to bless their ministry to be a blessing to others.

A husband and wife who are strong in the Lord Jesus Christ is a powerful couple to help strengthen those who are weak in their faith in the Lord.

A husband and wife who give Jesus the glory and praise for what He brought them through is a powerful couple in giving their testimonies about Jesus bringing them through their hard times together.

A husband and wife who put their trust in Jesus will have a peace of mind together for people to see them not worrying and complaining when things go wrong.

A husband and wife who are saved in Jesus is a powerful couple who the angels rejoice over.

A husband and wife who live for Jesus is a powerful couple who love each other, even if they just don't understand why the Lord is testing them in their marriage with the changes they go through together.

Love is Everything

Money is not everything.

Sex is not everything.

Success is not everything.

Achievements are not everything.

Awards are not everything.

Talents are not everything.

Love is everything.

Beauty is not everything.

Education is not everything.

Technology is not everything.

Science is not everything.

Medicine is not everything.

Love is everything.

Clothes are not everything.

Jewelry is not everything.

Skills are not everything.

The military is not everything.

Politics are not everything.

The government is not everything.

Computers are not everything.

Social media is not everything.

Fame is not everything.

Wealth is not everything.

Power is not everything.

Freedom is not everything.

Justice is not everything.

Equality is not everything.

The law is not everything.

Cars are not everything.

Trucks are not everything.

Airplanes are not everything.

Trains are not everything.

Pets are not everything.

Exercise is not everything.

Houses are not everything.

Love is everything.

Sports are not everything.

Greatness is not everything.

Genius is not everything.

Brilliance is not everything.

Intelligence is not everything.

Common sense is not everything.

Knowledge is not everything.

Wisdom is not everything.

Health is not everything.

Love is everything.

iPhones and smart phones are not everything.

Texting is not everything.

Facebook is not everything.

Instagram is not everything.

Jobs are not everything.

Entertainment is not everything.

Movies are not everything.

Love is everything.

Nature is not everything.

This world is not everything.

The universe is not everything.

Love is everything because love is God and God is love.

Books are not everything.

Music is not everything.

Boats are not everything.

Ships are not everything.

Traveling is not everything.

Vacations are not everything.

TVs are not everything.

Washers and dryers are not everything.

Air conditioners and heating units are not everything.

Love is everything that God is every day and we need God's love more than anything in this world.

Inventions are not everything.

Theories are not everything.

Mysteries are not everything.

Luck is not everything.

Phenomena are not everything.

Spiritual gifts are not everything.

Human beings are not everything.

Angels are not everything.

Love is everything that God gave to the world through His Son Jesus Christ, who demonstrated God's love in His perfect life and also in His death on the cross to save us from our sins when He rose from the grave, and that can't take away God's love from the righteous dead.

Video games are not everything.

FaceTime is not everything.

Parties are not everything.

Alcohol is not everything.

Drugs are not everything.

Cigarettes are not everything.

Guns are not everything.

Love is everything that is God who is love forever and ever.

Cities are not everything.

Nations are not everything.

Heroes are not everything.

War veterans are not everything.

Doctors are not everything.

Nurses are not everything.

Judges are not everything.

Lawyers are not everything.

Love is everything because love is from God.

Parents are not everything.

Children are not everything.

Hospitals are not everything.

Courthouses are not everything.

Businesses are not everything.

The church is not everything.

Love is everything because love begins with God, who created the heavens and earth with love.

Even in Our Body Language

If people don't do what we want them to do, then we may judge them, even in our body language and not talk to them.

If people don't respond to us in a good way when we talk to them, then we may judge them, even in our body language, and avoid talking to them again.

If people say words to us that we don't like, then we may judge people even in our body language by not even looking at them and acting like we don't see them.

If people don't talk about what we talk about, then we may judge them even in our body language and avoid them when we see them coming our way.

If people don't do what we do, then we may judge them even in our body language and avoid them because we don't want to be around them.

If people don't look like us, then we may judge them even in our body language and avoid them by not accepting them for looking different.

We can judge people even in our body language by avoiding talking to them if they are not on our educational level.

We can judge people even in our body language by avoiding people who speak a different language than us.

We can judge people in our body language that speaks louder than judging people in our words.

Jesus judges the heart, but we can be caught up in judging peoples' outward appearances.

Even in our body language we can judge people and be so wrong, but Jesus judges our hearts and is always right beyond our words of judging people and beyond our body language of judging people.

Doing Good to Others

Doing good to others can cause them to feel good.

Doing good to others can lift them up if they are feeling down.

Doing good to others can make their day to be good.

Doing good to others can give them a positive outlook on life.

Doing good to others can help them to be good.

Doing good to others can cause them to not give up.

Doing good to others can help them to see that there are good people in this world.

Doing good to others can help them to want to have a relationship with the Lord.

Doing good to others can help strengthen them in the Lord.

Doing good to others can put a smile on their faces.

Doing good to others can cheer them up.

Doing good to others can lift you and me up if we are feeling down.

Doing good to others can cause you and me to feel good.

Doing good to others can give you and me joy.

Doing good to others can give you and me a positive outlook on life.

Doing good to others can strengthen you and me in the Lord.

Doing good to others can help you and me to be good to ourselves.

Doing good to others can help heal their broken spirits.

Doing good to others can give them hope.

Doing good to others can help them to see that there is a God.

Doing good to others can save their souls from being lost.

Doing good to others can help them have a closer relationship with Jesus.

Doing good to others can help you and me to keep our eyes on Jesus, who is good to everyone and wants to save their souls from being lost in sin.

Doing good to others can help them to hold onto Jesus Christ in this troubled world.

God is Not Evil

God is not evil, even though God allows bad things to happen in this world.

You and I can't question God about to why He allows bad things to happen.

Who are we to question God, who is not evil because He gave us a free will to choose right from wrong?

The devil is the one who is evil and makes bad things happen in this world that he is the prince of.

God is good all the time, even though He allows bad things to happen for His reasons that are always good and fair.

We can believe that God is so wrong to allow bad things to happen, especially when they happen to people we believe don't deserve it.

The devil loves to make God look evil, even though it's the devil who is the evil one and he makes bad things happen in this world every day.

The devil has his human agents committing evil acts against anyone they can.

If God was evil, God would never have given us a free will to choose right from wrong.

God is not an evil, controlling God and He didn't create us to be robots who can't make choices ourselves.

Many people choose to do evil and cause good and innocent people to suffer, and the devil loves to see this.

God hates evil, because God is love.

We can't blame God for the bad things that happen in this sinful world when the devil and his fallen angels and human agents are to blame.

God will one day destroy them in hell's fire and brimstone.

The only thing we can blame God for is loving us whether we do right all the time or not.

God is love and God will be God, even though the devil loves to make God look evil because the devil can't be God, who is love.

There is no love in the devil.

It will be a strange act for God to destroy what He created.

If God makes something bad happen, we can believe that it's for God's good reason and no one can have a better reason than God.

What Can We Call Our Own?

What can we call our own, when tornadoes can take away everything that we have?

What can we call our own, when hurricanes can take away everything that we have?

What can we call our own, when floods can take away everything that we have?

What can we call our own, when earthquakes can take away everything that we have?

What can we call our own, when wars can take away everything that we have?

What can we call our own, when unemployment can take away everything that we have?

What can we call our own, when scammers can take away everything that we have?

What can we call our own, when illness can take away everything that we have?

What can we call our own, when misfortune can take away everything that we have?

What can we call our own, when poverty can take away everything that we have?

What can we call our own, when drugs can take away everything that we have?

What can we call our own, when alcohol can take away everything that we have?

What can we call our own, when God can take away everything that we have?

What can we call our own, when death can take you and me to the grave where we have nothing to own?

Death will own you and me until Jesus comes back again to set us free from death if we are saved in Him.

The only thing that we can truly call our own is our free will choices that no natural disasters, illness, misfortune or poverty can take away from us.

God will not take away our free will choice to choose, even if we lose everything that we have.

A Storm is Not Peaceful

Whenever a storm comes up, it can frighten us and make us be quiet and still until the storm is over.

Even the animals will be frightened when the storm comes up, and they will want to hide away until it's over.

A storm is not peaceful, and will be noisy outside of our house and inside of our house.

When the storm is over, there is peace up in the sky and down on the ground because we know that the storm is over and we can go about our daily business.

A storm is not peaceful.

There can be financial storms that rage in our bank accounts.

A storm is not peaceful.

There can be a mental storm that can rage in our minds.

A storm is not peaceful.

There can be an emotional storm that can rage in our hearts.

A storm is not peaceful.

There can be a spiritual storm that can rage in the church.

Whenever a storm comes up, it can frighten us no matter what kind of storm it might be.

A storm is not peaceful.

There can be an illness storm that can rage in our minds and bodies.

No matter what kind of storm rages, only Jesus Christ can truly calm the storm.

No matter what kind of storm rages, only Jesus Christ can give us a peace of mind in the storm.

No matter what kind of storm rages in our lives, the storm will obey Jesus Christ when He commands it to be at peace with us.

Jesus is a storm catcher who will stop a storm from coming our way if it is His will.

If Jesus allows a storm to come our way, then the storm is to test our faith in Him, even if Jesus allows the storm to take us to our deaths.

A storm is not peaceful; a storm is noisy to truly get our attention.

Jesus will sometimes have to use more than one storm to get our full attention on Him.

A storm can cause us to take our eyes off Jesus, just like Peter did, and begin to sink down in the water like Peter did when he looked at the storm and rugged waves and began to doubt that Jesus was more powerful than the storm.

Life is Victorious in the End

After a loved one dies and we grieve, things will go back to normal because life is victorious in the end.

After a tornado touches down on the ground and destroys everything in its path, things will go back to normal because life is victorious in the end.

After a hurricane blows down many buildings, things will go back to normal because life is victorious in the end.

After an earthquake breaks up the ground and crumbles down houses, things will go back to normal because life is victorious in the end.

After a wildfire burns up everything in its way, things will go back to normal because life is victorious in the end.

After a war kills many people and the war is over, things will go back to normal because life is victorious in the end.

After a deadly virus spreads across the land and kills many people and then scientists find an antidote for the virus, things will go back to normal because life is victorious in the end.

After the flood waters rise and get into peoples' houses and then flow back into the river, things will go back to normal because life is victorious in the end.

After God closes His probation on this sinful world and Jesus Christ comes back again to take all of His children to heaven, things will go back to the normal eternal life as if we never lived our lives being stained by sin.

After we live our life for Jesus Christ and die being saved in Jesus Christ, then Jesus will take us back to God's normal eternal life that is victorious in the end after this short life is over in this world that will pass away with all who lived a wicked life.

What Matters Most

What matters most is that you know yourself.

What matters most is that you believe in the good you do.

What matters most is what you want to accomplish in your life.

What matters most is that you tell the truth.

What matters most is how far you want to go in life.

What matters most is that you love yourself.

What matters most is that you live right by example.

What matters most is that you don't give up on yourself.

What matters most is that you know what you want to be.

What matters most is that you know what you want in your life.

What matters most is that you love everybody.

What matters most is that you have peace within yourself.

What matters most is that you are in control of yourself.

What matters most is that you believe in Jesus Christ.

What matters most is that you will confess and repent of your sins unto Jesus Christ.

What matters most is that you will deny yourself and pick up your cross and follow Jesus Christ.

What matters most is that you work out your own soul's salvation.

What matters most is that you will be a witness of Jesus Christ.

What matters most is that you are filled with the Holy Spirit.

What matters most is that you won't deny Jesus Christ.

What matters most is that you will use your spiritual gifts in the church.

What matters most is that you will go to church to worship Jesus Christ.

What matters most is that you will win souls to Jesus Christ.

What matters most is that you are saved in Jesus Christ.

What matters most is that you won't compromise the truth of God's holy word with false doctrine.

What matters most is you are faithful unto the Lord Jesus Christ.

What matters most is that you love Jesus and keep His Commandments.

What matters most is that you make the right choices in your life.

What matters most is that you won't let anyone or anything get between you and Jesus.

Can be a Deep, Mystical Unknown

The ocean can be a deep, mystical unknown with creatures down in the deepest parts on the ocean floor.

The outer space can be a deep, mystical unknown place with other worlds that we don't see because they may be billions of light years away from this world.

The cave can be a deep, mystical unknown place filled with the dark twenty-four hours around the clock.

Attraction can be a deep, mystical unknown of interest because you don't always know who is attracted to you wherever you go.

God's holy word can be a deep, mystical unknown truth because there is always a new truth to learn about God in His holy word.

Time can be a deep, mystical unknown of not really knowing when our time will end in this world.

You and I can be a deep, mystical unknown of human beings because we don't always know what we will say and we don't always know what we will do, especially on the spur of the moment.

Our minds can be a deep, mystical unknown of thoughts entering into our minds at any time.

Our hearts can be a deep, mystical unknown of what we may feel that can be good or bad feelings.

People can be a deep, mystical unknown of human beings because we always have a free will choice to choose right from wrong, but only God always knows who will choose to believe in His Son, Jesus Christ to be saved.

God can be a deep, mystical unknown God who will sometimes work in mysterious ways that you and I will not understand, but we can know that God is always right about whatever He does for us.

Tomorrow can be a deep, mystical unknown of not knowing if we will live to see tomorrow, which is not promised to us to live if it's not God's will.

The deep, mystical unknown of our trials that can come upon us when we are off guard, but God will not send us more hardships than we can handle with our love for His Son, Jesus Christ.

An unanswered prayer can be a deep, mystical unknown and only God knows what is best for you and me who don't know if we will be strong enough to handle an answered prayer.

The Ocean Of

The ocean of our thoughts runs very deep and our words bring them to the surface.

The ocean of our minds runs very deep and our choices bring it to the surface.

The ocean of our feelings runs very deep and our emotions bring it to the surface.

The ocean of our hearts runs very deep and our actions bring it to the surface.

The ocean of our lives runs very deep and our destiny brings it to the surface.

The ocean of our faith in Jesus runs very deep and our obedience brings it to the surface.

The ocean will always run very deep, but never deep enough for Jesus to not know everything on the bottom of the ocean floor.

No matter how deep our thoughts can be, Jesus can bring them to the surface as words to be a blessing to others.

No matter how deep our minds can be, Jesus can bring it to the surface of helping us to make the right choices.

No matter how deep our feelings can be, Jesus can bring them to the surface to help us to keep our emotions on track.

No matter how deep our hearts can be, Jesus can bring it to the surface and help us to have good actions every day.

No matter how deep our lives can be, Jesus can bring it to the surface of His goodness that leads us to repentance.

The ocean of our existence runs very deep, and only Jesus can bring it to the surface of His creation.

No matter how deep our existence can be, no evolution can take credit for it, no big bang theory can take credit.

Our existence is like one drop of water to Jesus who created all the oceans that run very deep in His creative mysteries and glory.

May Not Knock on Our Door

Another second may not knock on our door with the gift of life from God.

Another minute might not knock on our door with the gift of life from God.

Another hour might not knock on our door with the gift of life from God.

Another day might not knock on our door with the gift of life from God.

Another week might not knock on our door with the gift of life from God.

Another month might not knock on our door with the gift of life from God.

Another year might not knock on our door with the gift of life from God.

The reason why we are alive right now is because life has knocked on our door with God's mercy.

The reason why we are alive right now is because life has knocked on our door with God's approval to let us live today.

People will knock on our door and walk away if we don't open our door.

Life will knock on our door with God's goodness that won't walk away if we don't open our door right away.

God's goodness will keep on knocking on our door until we open it and repent and live for Jesus.

When on the spur of the moment even another second might not knock on the door of our souls, God can make sure that we will get a second chance to open our door and see that we have no excuse to take even a spur of the moment for granted.

The horror of death can crush our life-long dreams in only one second, but being alive is life from God who knocks on our door of choosing to live for Jesus or not choosing to live for Jesus every second of the day and night.

O Lord, You Put it in Us

O Lord, You put it in us to be up all day and sleep all night long.

O Lord, You also put it in the animals to be up all day and sleep all night long.

O Lord, You put it in us to reason things out before we say something and do something.

O Lord, You put it in us to feel emotions, both good and bad.

O Lord, You put it in us to sense things, both good and bad.

O Lord, You put it in animals to sense things, both good and bad.

O Lord, You put it in us to choose right from wrong.

O Lord, You put it in us to have a will to live.

O Lord, You put it in us to love.

O Lord, You put it in us to work.

O Lord, You put it in us to talk to one another.

O Lord, You put it in us to help one another.

O Lord, You put it in us to dream.

O Lord, You put it in us to hope.

O Lord, You put it in us to prosper.

O Lord, You put it in us to survive.

O Lord, You put it in us to love You and keep Your Commandments.

O Lord, You put it in us to choose to do good or do evil.

With Complete Trust

We can truly trust Jesus Christ with complete trust because He will never say wrong words to us or do anything wrong to us.

We can't put our complete trust in one another, because we can mean each other good and well and still say some wrong words.

We can only trust Jesus Christ.

With complete trust in Jesus, we know He will never say any bad words to us and will never do anything bad to us.

We can't put our complete trust in ourselves, because we can think bad about someone we don't even know, even though that person may be a good person.

We can't put our complete trust in our hearts that can have ill feelings against someone who hasn't done anything wrong to us.

We can only trust Jesus Christ completely because He will never cause us to have any doubts about His love for us, even on our bad days.

We can have complete trust in Jesus to lift us up out of our gloom that mistrusting people can cause us to feel.

We can't even put our complete trust in our loving dogs, because they can run out of the house as soon as we open the door.

We can't put our complete trust in this world that can take us through some changes that we don't understand.

We can only trust Jesus Christ completely every day, and know that Jesus won't take us through any changes that will be nonsense.

We know Jesus is always the same Jesus who will never deceive us to believe we are wrong about some people, when we are actually right about some people who mean us no good and will pretend to be on good terms with us.

Up and Down Like a Seesaw

O Lord, you knew I would be up and down like a seesaw, but I thank You, O Lord, for being patient with me as I follow You all the way in this sinful world.

O Lord, You knew I would be up and down like a seesaw, but I thank You for showing Your great mercy on me to wise up and do Your holy will like I need to do.

O Lord, You knew I would be up and down like a see saw, but I thank You for not giving up on me when I was living in my sins.

O Lord, You knew I would be up and down like a seesaw, but I thank You for not letting me fall off the seesaw of my hardships that I had to go through for You to mold and shape me into a new creature in You, my Lord and Savior Jesus Christ.

O Lord, You knew I would be up and down like a seesaw, but I truly thank You for watching over me and protecting me when I was on the devil's playground while I was on one end of the seesaw and the devil was on the other end.

O Lord, You knew I would be up and down like a seesaw even in the church, but I thank You for Your faithful children who didn't try to run me out of the church when I was up and down like a seesaw.

The Voices of Children

The voices of children can sound so sweet, even if they say something wrong.

The voices of children can be so innocent because little children have pure motives and intentions every day.

The voices of children are like sweet music to my ears when I hear them talk with so much innocence.

The voices of children are like heaven on earth to me because they are a blessing from God, even when they don't know what they're talking about.

God Loves the voices of children with an everlasting love.

Jesus Christ said, "Let the little children come to me, and do not hinder them, for the kingdom of heaven belongs to such as these."

The voices of children are not like the voices of adults, who can talk with grudging words; the voices of children talk with loving words.

Many adults should take the time to listen and hear the voices of children sounding so sweet and innocent, even if they don't know what they are talking about.

The voices of children are not like the voices of adults who can talk mean and hateful and depress people.

The voices of children can surely soothe a broken heart and cheer up a sad soul.

When little children play together, their voices sound so heavenly and divine because they have no grudges and strife like adults can have.

We adults need to listen to the voices of children and learn something good to hold onto.

Will Live Their Lives Like

A lot of people will live their lives like this life is the only life they can ever live.

A lot of people don't believe that there is a God who can give them an eternal life that they can live.

A lot of people will live their lives like this life is all they have to live, so they live it as they please and believe there is no God to judge them.

The worst kind of people are people who once believed in God and no longer believe anymore.

They live their lives like there is no eternal life that God will give to all who believe in His Son, Jesus Christ.

A lot of people believe that only this life can give them all of their hearts' desires and believe that there is no God who lives forever when they die.

A lot of people live their lives like there is no God who can't do anything for them.

They believe they are self-made and can do all things.

A lot of people will live their lives like luck, crossed fingers, magic, theories and mysteries are their power source for living, when it's truly God who gives life and will make life worth living unto Him for believing in his Son, Jesus Christ.

A lot of people will live their lives like there is no God to be above their consciousness and make them aware that there is a higher power.

A lot of people will want that higher power to spare their lives from death if they are in great danger and hoping for a miracle that they don't give God the praise for.

Their conscience is smeared in lies about there being no God.

A lot of people will live their lives like this is the only life to live for them.

They live by eyesight and for what they can get in this world that will one day pass away below the heavens on high were God has an eternal life to give to all who are saved in his Son, Jesus Christ.

A lot of people will live their lives like this life is the only life to live.

This is true for all who are lost in their sins.

Only the righteous will receive eternal life in Jesus Christ.

Spiritual Pollution

We know that air pollution is bad, but spiritual pollution is much worse in this world.

Spiritual pollution is believing that we are saved through grace and don't have to keep the Commandments of God.

Jesus says, "If you love Me, keep My Commandments."

Spiritual pollution is believing that there is no God, when the bible says that God created the heavens and the earth.

We can look at nature and see that there is a much higher intelligence than human beings.

Spiritual pollution is believing that after we die we go straight to heaven.

The bible says that Jesus Christ is coming back again to raise the righteous dead and change the righteous living from mortal to immortal and take them to heaven.

Hopefully you and I will be in that great number that no man can count.

Spiritual pollution is believing that Jesus Christ was only a prophet, when Jesus is the Son of God.

In the Garden of Eden, Jesus was in the creation of Adam and Eve because God had said, "Let us make them in Our likeness."

Spiritual pollution is believing that Sunday is the holy Sabbath day of rest, when Saturday is actually the holy Sabbath day of rest.

Saturday is the seventh day of the week when God finished all of His works and rested.

The seventh day of the week is Saturday, not Sunday.

Spiritual pollution is believing that we can eat whatever foods we want to eat.

God tells us in the bible not to eat unclean meats, which many people eat today.

Air pollution is bad, but spiritual pollution is much worst and causes our souls to be lost and one day burn up in fire and brimstone.

Debate

The devil loves to debate the bible scriptures to try to make the scriptures what he wants them to be.

The devil loves to misinterpret the scriptures to try to make the bible scriptures look like a lie.

The devil has his human agents who love to debate the bible scriptures and twist them up and turn their truth around to lies.

The devil has his human agents who will give their own interpretations of the bible scriptures because they reject the Holy Spirit who inspired holy men to write the bible scriptures given to them by God.

Debating the bible scriptures is of the devil who twisted God's words up to Eve who the devil lied to in the Garden of Eden.

People who love to debate the bible scriptures are not living by God's holy word because they reject them as truth that will set them free from the devil's lies.

The people who love to debate the bible scriptures will surely reap what they sow and it will show and tell in their lives.

Debating the bible scriptures is a normal thing for many people to do, but it is not normal to God who had given no misinterpretations to his holy men to write the bible scriptures to correct us in our errors.

It's the Heart that Moves God

It's the heart that moves God to forgiveness and joy.

Words don't move God to bless us if our heart is not in our words.

If we were blind and couldn't see, that wouldn't stop our hearts from moving God to give us spiritual eyes to see His love for us.

If we were deaf and couldn't hear, that wouldn't stop our hearts from moving God to give us spiritual ears to hear His Holy Spirit speaking to us down in our hearts.

If we were paralyzed and couldn't walk, it wouldn't stop our hearts from moving God to give us spiritual legs and feet to walk with Him down the pathway of His holy word.

It's the heart that moved God to repent that He made man, until he looked deep down into Noah's heart and that moved God to give Noah His grace.

Good deeds don't move God if our hearts aren't in it.

Our motives in our hearts must be pure to God, as well as our intentions.

Anyone can do a good deed and appear to be good, but God truly knows if our hearts are pure in motives and intentions when we do good deeds.

It's the heart that moves God, since our words can be full of hot air and cause God to frown at us.

It's the heart that moves God, since our actions can be deceptive and full of pretense that God truly sees and will judge.

It's the heart that moves God to justice and to give us freedom from lies, since actions can be a lie like a wolf in sheep's clothing doing good deeds with pretense.

Real Life Issues

There are Christians who are so caught up in bible scriptures that they have a hard time dealing with real life issues.

They tend to walk away from real life issues because it's much easier to want to know bible scriptures than to want to know how to deal with real life issues.

The Christians had to deal with real life issues back in the bible days, and Jesus dealt with real life issues that people had when He lived here on earth without sin.

It's always good to know the bible scriptures because they have their purpose to help us to deal with real life issues.

Jesus commands us to love our neighbors and deal with their real life issues from day to day.

Many Christians love to quote and talk about bible scriptures, but don't talk about real life issues that we all must live with while putting our trust in Jesus to give us the strength to deal with them.

There are many Christians who have no problem with the truth of God's holy word in the bible scriptures, but many Christians have a problem with the truth about real life issues as seen all through the bible from the book of Genesis to the book of Revelation.

God's prophets of old dealt with real life issues that people had as well as themselves, who had sins that caused them to have real life issues like everyone else.

There are Christians who are so caught up in the bible scriptures that they pretend like they don't have real life issues and they don't give testimonies about what Jesus brought them through in their lives.

Every child of God will have some real life issues because being a Christian won't stop us from having issues in our lives.

We can put our trust in Jesus to help us to deal with our real life issues that He won't let get the best of us for holding onto Him.

We Would be Lying to Ourselves

We would be lying to ourselves if we believe that we have no sins, because we were born in sin because of our sinful nature.

We would be lying to ourselves if we believe that we are perfect to have no sins to confess and repent of unto the Lord Jesus Christ.

If we have no sins, then Jesus would have no need to cleanse us from our sins.

If we have no sins, then Jesus would have had no need to come to this world and give up His life to save us from our sins.

We would be lying to ourselves if we live our lives like we have no sins when we also go to church to assemble ourselves together and pray to Jesus to forgive us of our sins.

If we have no sins, we won't be sinners saved through God's grace.

The only perfection that we have is through the righteousness of Jesus Christ, who is perfect to have no sins.

We would be lying to ourselves if we believe that we can't sin against God.

We have seen sins and we have unseen sins.

There are sins in our lives that we are aware of and there are sins in our lives that we are not aware of.

O Lord, we need Your Holy Spirit to convict us of our sins that we can commit against You and not feel guilty about it without Your Holy Spirit convicting us.

The church is for sinners to confess and repent and live for Jesus every day that God's Commandments will point out our sins to us.

God's law is for sinners like you and me who can break God's holy law and might not realize it.

We would be lying to ourselves if we say that we are perfect to have no sins, and if we believe that and say that, we are sinning against God.

We would be lying to ourselves if we believe that we have no sins and don't have to keep God's Commandments that are perfect, holy and righteous for all the world to keep after we give our lives unto the Lord

The Lord can't cleanse us of all of our past sins if we hold onto even one of them.

Even after we give our lives unto the Lord, we still have some present sins to confess and repent of unto the Lord because sanctification is a lifetime process.

For as long as we live, we will have to confess and repent of some sins unto the Lord.

We would be lying to ourselves if we believe that we have no sins to confess and repent of unto the Lord Jesus Christ.

We would be lying to ourselves if we believe that we don't break God's Commandments even in unseen ways.

We can lie to ourselves because we were born in sin and this causes us to lie to ourselves.

God will never lie to us because God cannot lie through His Son, Jesus Christ, who can make us perfect before God through His righteousness when our righteousness is like filthy rags on our best behavior every day.

Sin Will Show
No Respect of Persons

Sin doesn't care about you being a doctor because sin will cause you to be lost if you live in sin.

Sin doesn't care about you being a scientist because sin will cause you to be lost if you live in sin.

Sin doesn't care about you being an engineer because sin will cause you to be lost if you live in sin.

Sin will show no respect of persons.

Sin doesn't care about you being a model because sin will cause you to be lost if you live in sin.

Sin doesn't care about you being a actor because sin will cause you to be lost if you you live in sin.

Sin doesn't care about you being a aircraft pilot because sin will cause you to be lost if you live in sin.

Sin will show no respect of persons.

Sin doesn't care about you being a mother because sin will cause you to be lost if you live in sin.

Sin doesn't care about you being a father because sin will cause you to be lost if you live in sin.

Sin doesn't care about you being a husband because sin will cause you to be lost if you live in sin.

Sin doesn't care about you being a wife because sin will cause you to be lost if you live in sin.

Sin will show no respect of persons.

Sin doesn't care about you being a musician because sin will cause you to be lost if you live in sin.

Sin doesn't care about you being a singer because sin will cause you to be lost if you live in sin.

Sin doesn't care about you being a judge because sin will cause you to be lost if you you live in sin.

Sin doesn't care about you being a police officer because sin will cause you to be lost if you live in sin.

Sin will show no respect of persons.

Sin doesn't care about you being an athlete because sin will cause you to be lost if you live in sin.

Sin doesn't care about you being rich because sin will cause you to be lost if you live in sin.

Sin doesn't care about you being poor because sin will cause you to be lost if you live in sin.

Sin doesn't care about you being the president of the United States because sin will cause you to be lost if you live in sin.

Sin doesn't care about you being a pastor because sin will cause you to be lost if you live in sin.

Sin doesn't care about you being a teacher because sin will cause you to be lost if you live in sin.

Sin will show no respect of persons.

Sin doesn't care about you being a pope because sin will cause you to be lost if you live in sin.

Sin doesn't care about you being young because sin will cause you to be lost if you live in sin.

Sin doesn't care about you being old because sin will cause you to be lost if you live in sin.

Sin doesn't care about you being an author because sin will cause you to be lost if you live in sin.

Sin doesn't care about you being a lawyer because sin will cause you to be lost if you live in sin.

Sin doesn't care about you being a soldier because sin will cause you to be lost if you live in sin.

Sin doesn't care about you being a body builder because sin will cause you to be lost if you live in sin.

Sin doesn't care about you being a martial artist because sin will cause you to be lost if you live in sin.

Sin will show no respect of persons.

Sin doesn't care about you being a publisher because sin will cause you to be lost if you live in sin.

Sin doesn't care about you being a business owner because sin will cause you to be lost if you live in sin.

Sin doesn't care about you being a motivator because sin will cause you to be lost if you live in sin.

Sin doesn't care about you being a supervisor because sin will cause you to be lost if you live in sin.

Sin will show no respect of persons.

Sin doesn't care about you being a nurse because sin will cause you to be lost if you live in sin.

Sin doesn't care about you being a psychiatrist because sin will cause you to be lost if you live in sin.

Sin doesn't care about you being a genius because sin will cause you to be lost if you live in sin.

Sin doesn't care about you being educated because sin will cause you to be lost if you live in sin.

Sin doesn't care about you being ignorant because sin will cause you to be lost if you live in sin.

Sin will show no respect of persons and Jesus Christ will show no respect of persons to save anyone from being lost in sin if we confess and repent of our sins and live a renewed life in loving Him and keeping His Commandments that point out our sins to us.

Running Our Mouths Too Much

Running our mouths too much can get us into trouble.

Running our mouths too much can give us a bad name.

Running our mouths too much can ruin our good name.

Running our mouths too much can cause us to make enemies.

Running our mouths too much can shorten our lives.

Running our mouths too much can hurt other people's reputations.

Running our mouths too much can cause people to not trust us.

Running our mouths too much can cause people to feel uncomfortable.

Running our mouths too much can cause people to feel bored.

Running our mouths too much can cause people to question us.

Running our mouths too much can cause people to not want to be around us.

Running our mouths too much can scare people away from us.

It's never a good thing to run our mouths too much, even in the church because the Lord wants us to show temperance in all things.

That's Just the Way it Is

If God allowed you to be tall, then that's just the way it is.

If God allowed you to be short, then that's just the way it is.

If God allowed you to be big, then that's just the way it is.

If God allowed you to be small, then that's just the way it is.

If God allowed you to be white, then that's just the way it is.

If God allowed you to be brown, then that's just the way it is.

If God allowed you to be black, then that's just the way it is.

If God allowed you to be a genius, then that's just the way it is.

If God allowed you to be educated, then that's just the way it is.

If God allowed you to be of average intelligence, then that's just the way it is.

If God allowed you to be smart, then that's just the way it is.

If God allowed you to be a boy, then that's just the way it is.

If God allowed you to be a girl, then that's just the way it is.

If God allowed you to be man, then that's just the way it is.

If God allowed you to be woman, then that's just the way it is.

God doesn't make mistakes, so we are all what God wants us to be.

If God allowed you to be a man, then why would you want to change that because God allowed you to be a man.

If God allowed you to be a woman, then why would you want to change that because God allowed you to be a woman.

God doesn't make mistakes.

You and I can make mistakes that God will frown at and shake His head at us.

If God allowed you to have male body parts, then that's just the way it is.

If God allowed you to have female body parts, then that's just the way it is.

God doesn't make mistakes about who He allowed us to be.

If God allowed you be beautiful, then that's just the way it is.

If God allowed you be attractive, then that's just the way it is.

If God allowed you be handsome, then that's just the way it is.

If God allowed you be average looking, then that's just the way it is.

If God allowed you be unattractive, then that's just the way it is.

You and I must accept the way that God allowed us to be and live with it, because God doesn't make mistakes about who He allows us to be.

If God allowed you to be rich, then that's just the way it is.

If God allowed you to be upper middle class, then that's just the way it is.

If God allowed you to be lower middle class, then that's just the way it is.

If God allowed you to be poor, then that's just the way it is.

If God allowed you to be very talented, then that's just the way it is.

If God allowed you to be very skillful, then that's just the way it is.

If God allowed you to be talkative, then that's just the way it is.

If God allowed you to be quiet, then that's just the way it is.

God will allow us to be bad, but He is against it.

God will allow us to live in sin, but He is against it.

God will allow us to be lost in our sins, but He is against it.

Just because God allowed us to have a free will to make choices in our lives, it doesn't mean that God will go along with every word we say and everything we do, and that's just the way it is with God.

If God allowed you to live a long life, whether you are good or bad, then that is just the way it is with God, who always knows what's best for you and me.

When Trouble Keeps Coming Your Way

When trouble keeps coming your way, you can only hope that Jesus will answer your prayers.

When trouble keeps coming your way, you can only hope that Jesus will allow you to live through it without having a heart attack or stroke.

Whether you believe in Jesus or not, you can hope to survive troubled times that keep coming your way.

The Lord may allow trouble to keep coming your way so you will humble yourself unto Him and acknowledge that you need Him to get rid of the troubled times in your life.

The Lord may allow trouble to keep coming your way so you will want to change from your selfish ways and follow Him who is the way, truth and life.

The Lord may allow trouble to keep coming your way so you will want to depend on His strength to keep you strong through your troubled times that will drain you and your strength will fail you.

When trouble keeps coming your way, you can only hope that you are rooted and grounded in Jesus because if you are not your troubles will surely get the best of you and you will fall apart mentally, emotionally and most of all, spiritually.

When trouble keeps coming your way and my way, we can choose to trust Jesus to remove our troubles that have no power over our free will for us to keep our eyes on Jesus who can give us the victory over all of our troubles that are like a little hangnail for Jesus to clip.

Standing Beside the Road of Life

Are we standing beside the road of life with our arms stretched out and our thumbs up asking the world to stop by and pick us up to take us to our dreams?

Are we standing beside the road of life with our arms stretched out and our thumbs up asking the world to stop by and pick us up to take us to success?

Are we standing beside the road of life with our arms stretched out and our thumbs up asking the world to stop by and pick us up to take us to what we wish for?

Are we standing beside the road of life with our arms stretched out and our thumbs up asking the world to stop by and pick us up to take us to happiness?

Are we standing beside the road of life with our arms stretched out and our thumbs up asking the world to stop by and pick us up to take us to freedom?

Are we standing beside the road of life with our arms stretched out and our thumbs up asking the world to stop by and pick us up to take us to whatever we want?

We can surely stand beside the road of life with our arms stretched out and our thumbs up asking for Jesus to stop by and pick us up to take us to His love, mercy and truth.

We can surely stand beside the road of life with our arms stretched out and our thumbs up asking Jesus to stop by and pick us up to take us to His salvation.

We can surely stand beside the road of life with our arms stretched out and our thumbs up asking Jesus to stop by and pick us up to take us to heaven when Jesus comes back again on the clouds of glory.

It's Not Easy On

It's not easy on many people who live alone, especially senior citizens who have slowed down and can't do a lot of things like they could when they were young.

It's not easy on many old people to live alone because they need to be taken care of to ease their burdens of everyday living in their houses all alone.

It's not easy on many people who don't live alone because the people they live with are not doing right.

Many people who don't live alone wish they could live alone so they could have a peace of mind.

It's not easy on people who are living in their troubled times because many people are unequally yoked when God and the devil cannot be on one accord in the same house.

It's not easy to live with someone who is not a Christian and just doesn't want to love Jesus and keep His Commandments.

Many people don't like living alone, but other people would rather live alone than live with someone who is living for the devil.

If you are living in the same house with people who love you and respect you for being a Christian, then they are a blessing from the Lord for you to live with and be a living example for them.

It's not easy on any Christian, whether they live alone or don't live alone, whether they're old, middle aged or young when the devil is all about trying to discourage every Christian and make them give up on their faith in Jesus.

The devil makes it easy on people who he can use to make it hard on you and me for being a Christian.

The devil can also use his human agents to make it easy on you and me to overlook what we don't see to be a sin that is very clever to set up traps for us to fall into when we don't see it coming our way.

The Typos in Our Lives

If we don't let Jesus correct the typos in our lives, then our names will not be in the book of life.

If we judge people, we have a typo in our lives.

If we believe that we are better than other people, we have a typo in our lives.

If we are prejudiced against people of other races, we have a typo in our lives.

If we confess and repent of our sins, Jesus can correct the typos in our lives.

If we gossip about people, we have a typo in our lives.

If we are rude to people, we have a typo in our lives.

If we are mean to people, we have a typo in our lives.

If we talk bad about people, we have a typo in our lives.

If we pray to Jesus with a pure, sincere heart, Jesus can correct the typos in our lives.

If we are proud and look down on those who are less fortunate, we have a typo in our lives.

If we tell lies on people, we have a typo in our lives.

If we treat people bad, we have a typo in our lives.

If we don't eat the right foods, we have a typo in our lives.

If we talk too much, we have a typo in our lives.

If we live our lives unto Jesus every day, He can correct the typos in our lives.

If we don't love one another in the church, we have a typo in our lives.

If we don't forgive people, we have a typo in our lives.

If we ruin someone's good name, we have a typo in our lives.

If we deceive people, we have a typo in our lives.

If we are not serious about doing God's will, we have a typo in our lives.

If we compromise God's holy word with false doctrines, we have a typo in our lives.

If we know to do right and don't do right, we have a typo in our lives.

There are many books that have typos in them and the authors may not see every typo until the book is published for people to read.

If a book is good to read, even with a typo in it, there are people who will overlook the typo and not consider it a bad thing in the book.

Jesus will not overlook the typos in our lives, regardless of people reading you and me to be good people.

If we don't surrender our hearts to Jesus and let Him correct the typos in our lives, then our names will be blotted out of the book of life that has no typos in it for the angels to read and know that there won't be any misspelled saints in heaven.

Living in Paradise

I believed that I was living in paradise when I was in the army and stationed in Hawaii.

I remember when I was flying in the United 747 aircraft and looked out the window and saw the beautiful green hills and waterfalls.

I also remember seeing the beautiful navy blue pacific ocean waters that captivated my attention during my flight to Hawaii.

I believed that I was living in paradise when I got on the bus leaving Scofield barracks and going to Waikiki with my friends on the weekends when I was off-duty.

Waikiki was like a paradise with beautiful Hawaiian women looking like heaven on earth, along with the mystical park sitting so close to the beautiful white beach sand.

The Hawaiian native Samoan men and women were friendly and like angels on earth to me.

They were so good to be around and smoke pot with.

I wasn't a Christian at that time, but I truly felt like I was in heaven on earth when I was stationed in Hawaii.

That was the most beautiful place I have been to in my life.

If Hawaii can be like a paradise and other places here on earth can too, then what about the real paradise in Heaven that Jesus wants to take us to when He comes back again?

We just can't imagine what heaven is like, but we can be very sure that heaven is a paradise where there is no sin.

God will create a new heaven and a new earth that will be paradise for all who are saved in Jesus Christ who is paradise to our souls for being saved in Him.

Paradise would not be paradise without Jesus, who allowed Hawaii to be like a paradise as well as other tropical islands that belong to Jesus, who also owns all the world, all the heavens and all the other worlds.

We Can Never Learn Enough About

We can never learn enough about God's love that we can never get enough of.

We can never learn enough about God's mercy that we can never get enough of.

We can never learn enough about God's grace that we can never get enough of.

We can never learn enough about God's patience that we can never get enough of.

We can never learn enough about God's peace that we can never get enough of.

We can never learn enough about God's mystery that we can never get enough of.

We can never learn enough about God's goodness that we can never get enough of.

We can never learn enough about God's holy word that we can never get enough of.

We can never learn enough about God's Son, Jesus Christ, who we can never get enough of.

We can never learn enough about God's Holy Spirit who we can never get enough of.

We can never learn enough about God's creations that we can never get enough of.

We can never learn enough about God's existence that we can never get enough of.

We can never learn enough about God who we can never get enough of.

We can never learn enough about God's children who we can never get enough of.

We can never learn enough about God's church that we can never get enough of.

We can never learn enough about God's glory that we can never get enough of.

We can never learn enough about God's heaven that we will never get enough of when we live in heaven one day with God and His Son, Jesus Christ, and Holy Spirit, along with all of His angels.

We can never learn enough about God's Son, Jesus Christ's victory over death and the grave that Jesus was risen from that we can never get enough of.

We can never learn enough about God's Son, Jesus Christ, who is our Lord and Savior who we can never get enough of for being saved in Him.

We can never learn enough about God's Son, Jesus Christ, who will cleanse us from our sins if we confess and repent of our sins that we can never get enough of to be like Jesus.

We can never learn enough about God's Son, Jesus Christ, and worship Him who we can never get enough of.

We can never learn enough about God's Son, Jesus Christ, who kept God's Commandments that we can never get enough of.

We can never learn enough about God's judgment that we can never get enough of.

We can never learn enough about God's protection that we can never get enough of.

We can never learn enough about God's miracles that we can never get enough of.

We can never learn enough about the ministry of God's Son, Jesus Christ; we can never get enough of that.

We can never learn enough about God's Son, Jesus Christ, and His holiness, righteousness, and complete perfection that we can never get enough of.

Without Your Holy Spirit, O Lord

Without Your Holy Spirit, O Lord, I don't know how to pray to You.

Without Your Holy Spirit, O Lord, I don't' know how to be a witness of You.

Without Your Holy Spirit, O Lord, I don't know how to talk about You.

Without Your Holy Spirit, O Lord, I don't know how to think about You.

Without Your Holy Spirit, O Lord, I don't know how to love You.

Without Your Holy Spirit, O Lord, I don't know how to live right unto You.

Without Your Holy Spirit, O Lord, I don't know how to obey You.

Without Your Holy Spirit, O Lord, I don't know how to believe in You.

Without Your Holy Spirit, O Lord, I don't know how to deny myself and pick up my cross and follow You.

Without Your Holy Spirit, O Lord, I don't know how to be like You, my Lord and Savior Jesus Christ.

It's your Holy Spirit who connects me to You, O Lord.

It's your Holy Spirit who reaches out to me first before I make any choice to confess and repent of my sins unto You, O Lord.

It's your Holy Spirit who convicts me to live for You, O Lord.

Without Your Holy Spirit, O Lord, I don't know how to feel guilty for sinning against You, O Lord.

Without Your Holy Spirit, O Lord, I don't know how to put my hope in You, O Lord.

Without Your Holy Spirit, O Lord, I don't know how to accept Your blood that was shed on the cross that You died on to save me from my sins as if I was the only sinner.

It's Your Holy Spirit who lets me know that no one can ever love me more than You, My Lord Jesus Christ.

It's Your Holy Spirit who lets me know that only You, my Lord Jesus, are my redeemer and my salvation.

Will Lead Us in the Right Direction

Pure motives in our hearts will lead us in the right direction for us to get near to the heart of God.

Confession and repentance will lead us in the right direction for us to get near to the heart of God.

The holy word of God will lead us in the right direction for us to get near to the heart of God.

The Ten Commandments will lead us in the right direction for us to get near to the heart of God.

Prayer will lead us in the right direction for us to get near to the heart of God.

Faith in Jesus will lead us in the right direction for us to get near to the heart of God.

Hope in Jesus Christ will lead us in the right direction for us to get near to the heart of God.

Loving Jesus Christ will lead us in the right direction for us to get near to the heart of God.

Loving one another will lead us in the right direction for us to get near to the heart of God.

Our good and pure works for Jesus Christ will lead us in the right direction for us to get near to the heart of God.

Our obedience unto Jesus Christ will lead us in the right direction for us to get near to the heart of God.

Most of all, the Holy Spirit will lead us in the right direction for us to get near to the heart of God.

Most of all, the cross will lead us in the right direction for us to get near to the heart of God.

Most of all, Jesus Christ will lead us in the right direction for us to get near to the heart of God who so loved the world that He gave His only begotten Son, that whosoever believeth in Him should not perish but have everlasting life.

To the New Jerusalem Holy City

All the traffic lights will stay green for the traffic of the saints to keep moving non-stop to the new Jerusalem holy city.

There will be no yield signs to be cautious of and everyone will have plenty of space to enter into the new Jerusalem holy city.

There will be no speed limit signs because all the saints will flow smoothly into the new Jerusalem holy city.

There will be no bumper to bumper traffic because all the saints will keep their distance on the road to the new Jerusalem holy city.

There will be no accidents because Jesus will direct the traffic of the saints to enter into the new Jerusalem holy city.

There will be no cameras taking pictures because no holy saint of God will be speeding on road leading to the new Jerusalem holy city if we are in that number of saints that no one can count except Jesus.

Jesus is building the new Jerusalem holy city for all the saints to enter into one day soon when Jesus comes back again with all the angels in heaven.

There will be no bumps and potholes on the road, and there will be no yellow or white lines on the road because all the saints will stay in their lanes and not speed past one another on the road leading them, and you and me, to the new Jerusalem holy city in heaven.

Your God-Given Talents

Don't let anyone in your family discourage you from using your God-given talents.

Don't let anyone in your neighborhood discourage you from using your God-given talents.

Don't let anyone on your job discourage you from using your God-given talents.

Don't let anyone in your circle of friends discourage you from using your God-given talents.

Don't let anyone in your city discourage you from using your God-given talents.

Don't let anyone in your state discourage you from using your God-given talents.

Don't let anyone in your nation discourage you from using your God-given talents.

Don't let anyone in this world discourage you from using your God-given talents.

Don't let anyone in your life discourage you from using your God-given talents.

Don't discourage yourself from using your God-given talents.

God has given you and me talents to uplift His holy name.

God has given you and me talents to glorify Him.

Don't let the devil discourage you from using your God-given talents.

Our talents are God's masterpiece work for the angels in heaven to be amazed that God can use us for His holy purpose.

If you and I use our God-given talents for the devil, he will surely curse our lives sooner or later.

If you and I use our God-given talents for the devil, he will bring us down to nothing good sooner or later.

Don't let anybody discourage you from using your God-given talents that God didn't give to you to use for selfish ambitions.

Lucifer used his God-given talents in heaven for selfish ambitions that caused him and his fallen angels to be kicked out of heaven where only God is worthy to be worshipped above talents that are small things to God to give to us and also take away.

Invisible but Become Visible

Thoughts are invisible but become visible through our actions.

Words are invisible but become visible through our actions.

Feelings are invisible but become visible through our actions.

God is invisible but becomes visible through His love.

Words are invisible but became visible through his Son, Jesus Christ when He lived here on earth without sin.

God is invisible but becomes visible through the truth of His holy word.

God is invisible but becomes visible in a Christian's life.

God is invisible but becomes visible through His mercy.

God is invisible but becomes visible through His grace.

God is invisible but becomes visible through His miracles.

God is invisible but becomes visible through His justice.

God is invisible but becomes visible in our prayers.

God is invisible but becomes visible in worship.

God is invisible but becomes visible in His wisdom.

God is invisible but becomes visible in His goodness.

God is invisible but becomes visible in temperance.

God is invisible but becomes visible in peace.

God is invisible but becomes visible in His granting us a second chance.

God is invisible but becomes visible in our good health.

God is invisible but becomes visible in prosperity.

God is invisible but becomes visible in dreams.

God is invisible but becomes visible in visions.

God is invisible but becomes visible in prophecy.

God is invisible but becomes visible in allowing us to see this day.

God is invisible but becomes visible in all of His prophets of old.

God is invisible but becomes visible in hope.

God is invisible but becomes visible in victory.

God is invisible but becomes visible in protection.

God is invisible but becomes visible in His control over all things.

God is invisible but becomes visible when He works things out for us.

From a Long Ways In

O Lord, You brought me from a long ways in showing Your mercy on me.

O Lord, You brought me from a long ways in cleansing me from my past sins.

O Lord, You brought me from a long ways in having faith in You.

O Lord, You brought me from a long ways in worshipping You.

O Lord, You brought me from a long ways in putting my trust in You.

O Lord, You brought me from a long ways in holding onto You.

O Lord, You brought me from a long ways in keeping my eyes on You.

O Lord, You brought me from a long ways in praying to You.

O Lord, You brought me from a long ways in giving testimonies about what You brought me through.

O Lord, You brought me from a long ways in going through trials for Your holy name sake.

O Lord, You brought me from a long ways in confessing and repenting of my sins unto You.

O Lord, You brought me from a long ways in keeping Your Sabbath day holy unto You.

O Lord, You brought me from a long ways in Your amazing grace.

O Lord, You brought me from a long ways in denying myself and picking up my cross to follow You.

O Lord, You brought me from a long ways in keeping me in my right mind.

O Lord, You brought me from a long ways in keeping me in good health.

O Lord, You brought me from a long ways in eating Your spiritual meat.

O Lord, You brought me from a long ways in assembling together with my spiritual brothers and sisters in the household of faith to worship You and give You all the glory and praise.

O Lord, You brought me from a long ways in loving You and keeping Your Commandments.

O Lord, You brought me from a long ways in having a relationship with You.

O Lord, You brought me from a long ways in using my spiritual gifts to edify the church that You are the head of.

O Lord, You brought me from a long ways in spiritually maturing in You.

O Lord, You brought me from a long ways in not laying up my treasures in the world.

O Lord, You brought me from a long ways in not making this world my home.

O Lord, You brought me from a long ways in yielding to Your Holy Spirit.

O Lord, You brought me from a long ways in not holding grudges.

O Lord, You brought me from a long ways in loving everybody the same.

O Lord, You brought me from a long ways in waiting on You to work things out in my life.

O Lord, You brought me from a long ways in setting me free from the devil's lies.

O Lord, You brought me from a long ways in giving me the victory over my obstacles in life.

O Lord, You brought me from a long ways in keeping me alive to see this day for me to give You the honor, glory and praise.

People Would Rather See

It's always good to talk about Jesus, but people would rather see you and me being like Jesus.

People would rather see you and me being kind like Jesus.

People would rather see you and me being gentle like Jesus.

People would rather see you and me being humble like Jesus.

People would rather see you and me being joyful like Jesus.

People would rather see you and me being temperant like Jesus.

People would rather see you and me being faithful like Jesus.

People would rather see you and me being trustworthy like Jesus.

People would rather see you and me being loving like Jesus.

People would rather see you and me living right like Jesus.

You and I need the Holy Spirit to help us to be like Jesus.

We can't be like Jesus on our own strength.

We can't be like Jesus on our own intellect.

It's always good to spread the gospel of Jesus Christ, but people would rather see you and me living the gospel of Jesus Christ every day.

People would rather see you and me giving them a helping hand like Jesus.

I Want to be Caught Up in You, O Lord

I want to be caught up in You, O Lord, not caught up in myself.

I want to be caught up in You, O Lord, not caught up in anyone else.

I want to be caught up in You, O Lord, not caught up in what is going on in this world.

I want to be caught up in You, O Lord, not caught up in in the church.

I want to be caught up in You, O Lord, not caught up in material things.

I want to be caught up in You, O Lord, not caught up in how You are blessing me.

I want to be caught up in You, O Lord, not caught up in the spiritual gifts you have given me.

I want to be caught up in You, O Lord, not caught up in temporary things.

I want to be caught up in You, my Lord and Savior Jesus Christ, who is eternal for me to stay caught up in and never get disappointed.

Just Because You Are

Just because you are educated, it doesn't exempt you from going through any trials for Jesus' name sake.

Just because you are beautiful, it doesn't exempt you from going through any trials for Jesus' name sake.

Just because you are old, it doesn't exempt you from going through any trials for Jesus' name sake.

Just because you are young, it doesn't exempt you from going through any trials for Jesus' name sake.

Just because you are successful, it doesn't exempt you from going through any trials for Jesus' name sake.

Just because you are rich, it doesn't exempt you from going through any trials for Jesus' name sake.

Just because you are good, it doesn't exempt you from going through any trials for Jesus' name sake.

Just because you are healthy, it doesn't exempt you from going through any trials for Jesus' name sake.

Just because you are Christian, it doesn't exempt you from going through any trials for Jesus' name sake.

Just because you are filled with the Holy Spirit, it doesn't exempt you from going through any trials for Jesus' name sake.

Just because you are saved in Jesus, it doesn't exempt you from going through any trials for Jesus' name sake.

Going through trials for Jesus' holy name sake is something that we must do to be like Jesus, who went through hardships to save you and me from our sins.

Jesus went through the hardship of shedding His blood and giving up His life on the cross to pay our price and redeem us back to God.

If You

If you lay up your treasures in this world, soon or later you will get disappointed.

If you lay up your treasures in this world, soon or later you will get deceived.

If you lay up your treasures in this world, soon or later you will get let down.

If you lay up your treasures in this world, soon or later you will get your heart broken.

If you lay up your treasures in this world, soon or later you will get discouraged.

If you lay up your treasures in this world, soon or later you will get what's coming to you.

If you lay up your treasures in this world, soon or later you will get into trouble.

If you lay up your treasures in this world, soon or later you will get into foolishness.

If you lay up your treasures in this world, soon or later you will find sorrow.

If you lay up your treasures in this world, soon or later you will find emptiness.

If you lay up your treasures in this world, soon or later you will get worried.

If you lay up your treasures in heaven, soon or later you will get a peace of mind.

If you lay up your treasures in heaven, soon or later you will get joy.

If you lay up your treasures in heaven, soon or later you will get contentment.

If you lay up your treasures in heaven, soon or later you will get eternal security.

Will Get Angry at the Lord

Many people will get sick and get angry at the Lord.

Many people will go through hardships and get angry at the Lord.

Many people will lose everything that they have and get angry at the Lord.

The Lord may allow us to get sick to humble us so we acknowledge Him to be our greatest healer.

The Lord may allow us to go through hardships to make us strong in holding onto Him to bring us through those hardships.

The Lord may allow us to lose everything we have so He can mold and shape us to be all He will have us to be in glorifying His holy name.

Many people get angry at the Lord if bad things happen to them.

The Lord knows what it will take to save us from being lost in our sins.

We can easily believe that we are sanctified and filled with the Holy Spirit, but Jesus is the One who must take us through the fire of our trials to make us be more and more like Him who we should never be angry at.

If things don't go our way, we should not be angry at Jesus Christ, our Lord and Savior, because He always knows what it will take to remind us that we need to confess and repent of our sins and live for Him all the way because halfway won't do.

Many people will lose their loved ones and get angry at the Lord Jesus Christ who gives our deceased loved ones eternal life if they are saved in Him.

Every

Every teacher wants to have good students.

Every doctor wants to have good patients.

Every surgeon wants to have a good operation.

Every lawyer wants to win their courtroom case.

Every musician wants to play good music.

Every preacher wants to preach a good sermon.

Every child wants to have loving parents.

Every parent wants to have obedient children.

Every chef wants to cook good food.

Every business owner wants to make big profits.

Every home buyer wants to own their home.

Every pilot wants to fly to their destination.

Every driver wants to drive on a road.

Every soldier must wear a uniform on duty.

Every man, woman, boy and girl wants to be in good health.

Every dog will bark.

Every cat will meow.

Every snake will crawl.

Every bird will fly.

Every fool wants to do their own will.

Every fool will be a slave to sin.

Every real, true Christian will love Jesus and keep His Commandments.

Every real, true Christian is saved in Jesus Christ.

Every real, true Christian will go to heaven.

Every real, true Christian will love everybody.

Every angel in heaven will rejoice over one sinner who confesses and repents of his or her sins and lives for Jesus with a whole heart.

Speeding on the Roads of Life

Many people are speeding on the roads of life for being murderers.

Many people are speeding on the roads of life for being thieves.

Many people are speeding on the roads of life for being child molesters.

Many people are speeding on the roads of life for being rapists.

Many people are speeding on the roads of life for being liars.

Many people are speeding on the roads of life for being prostitutes.

Many people are speeding on the roads of life for being homosexuals.

Many people are speeding on the roads of life for being fornicators.

Many people are speeding on the roads of life for being adulterers.

Many people are speeding on the roads of life for being unfaithful to their spouses.

Many people are speeding on the roads of life for having children out of wedlock.

Many people are speeding on the roads of life for being pimps.

Many people are speeding on the roads of life for being greedy for worldly gain.

Many people are speeding on the roads of life for being gossipers.

Many people are speeding on the roads of life for holding grudges.

Many people are speeding on the roads of life for being hypocrites in the church.

Many people are speeding on the roads of life for being foolish.

Many people are speeding on the roads of life for being proud.

Many people are speeding on the roads of life for being deceivers.

Many people are speeding on the roads of life for being against God.

Many people are speeding on the roads of life for being the devil's human agents.

Many people are speeding on the roads of life for being lost in their sins.

God will give His speeding ticket of eternal death to all who don't believe in His Son, Jesus Christ, who is the only one who can throw our speeding ticket out of God's courtroom if we confess and repent of our sins and love and obey Him on the roads of life.

Many people are speeding on the roads of life for being prejudiced.

Many people are speeding on the roads of life for being abusers.

Many people are speeding on the roads of life for being pretenders.

Only Jesus can pardon our speeding ticket if we wise up and love Him and keep His Commandments.

We all fall short of the glory of God and will get a speeding ticket on the roads of life.

There are People Who

There are people who will not obey the rules in the neighborhood where they live.

There are people who will not obey the laws in the country where they live.

There are people who Just don't want to do what is right by the rules and laws in this world.

There is a higher law in the church where there are people who will not obey the law of God.

The law of God is above the laws of men that may not always be right to obey.

There are some laws of men that are not in line with the law of God.

God's holy law is always right and perfect to obey every day.

There are people who will protest against the government's laws if the laws are not right with them.

There are people who try to do away with God's holy law, even in many churches.

In many churches, there are people who believe that they don't have to obey God's holy law because of being saved through grace, but the law is God's character in Jesus Christ, who obeyed God's law when He lived on earth without sin.

To Love One Another Deeply

The Lord says for us to love one another deeply, but we all do fall short of loving one another deeply in the church.

We all are guilty of loving some of our spiritual brothers and sisters more than others, especially if they are more loving toward you and me.

We all are guilty of loving some of our spiritual brothers and sisters more than others, especially if they are more supportive of you and me.

The Lord says for us to love one another deeply in the church, regardless of who might be against us in the church.

If we don't love one another deeply, then how can we love Jesus deeply when Jesus loves everybody deeply with His everlasting love?

We surely need Jesus Christ, our Lord and Savior, to help us to love one another deeply because anything less than loving one another deeply will surely cause us to have some ill feelings toward one another in the church.

We all need to be loved deeply, and that is why the Lord says to love one another deeply so that the people of the world will see that we have deep love for one another in the church.

Nobody in the church should be left out of being loved deeply, and showing respect of persons will surely cause ill feelings to spread like a wildfire in the church.

It won't kill anyone to love everybody deeply in the church that Jesus Christ is the head of and will give us our reward for loving one another deeply regardless of our differences that Jesus can bring together on one accord in Him.

Jesus Doesn't Need Us

Jesus doesn't need us, because we will make some mistakes.

We need Jesus because He doesn't make any mistakes.

Jesus doesn't need us, because we won't say all the right words.

We need Jesus because He will say all the right words.

Jesus doesn't need us, because we won't do everything right.

We need Jesus because He will do everything right.

Jesus doesn't need us, because we have some flaws.

We need Jesus because He has no flaws.

Jesus doesn't need us, because we have sins to confess and repent of.

We need Jesus because He has no sins.

Jesus doesn't need us, because we were born in sin.

We need Jesus because He is sinless.

Jesus doesn't need us, because our lives are short-lived.

We need Jesus because He is the eternal life.

Jesus doesn't need us, because we can't save ourselves from being lost.

We need Jesus because He will save us from being lost in our sins if we believe in Him.

If we believe that Jesus needs us, then we are only fooling ourselves.

The Only True

The only true joy that I will get is from You, O Lord.

The only true peace that I will get is from You, O Lord.

The only true wisdom that I will get is from You, O Lord.

The only true compassion that I will get is from You, O Lord.

The only true strength that I will get is from You, O Lord.

The only true forgiveness that I will get is from You, O Lord.

The only true comfort that I will get is from You, O Lord.

The only true support that I will get is from You, O Lord.

The only true encouragement that I will get is from You, O Lord.

The only true motivation that I will get is from You, O Lord.

The only true victory that I will get is from You, O Lord.

The only true care that I will get is from You, O Lord.

The only true fairness that I will get is from You, O Lord.

The only true freedom that I will get is from You, O Lord.

The only true love that I will get is from You, my Lord and Savior Jesus Christ.

The only true spiritual growth that I will get is from You, my Lord and Savior Jesus Christ.

There are People Who Don't Want To

There are people who don't want to see you move up in your life.

There are people who don't want you to make any improvements in your life.

There are people who will try to get in your way to keep you from climbing up the ladder.

There are people who don't want to see you prosper in your life.

There are people who don't want to see you do better in your life.

There are people who don't care if you are lost in your sins.

There are people who don't want to see you do better than them.

There are people who would rather see you doing bad than doing good.

There are people who don't want to see you being in good health.

There are people who know you and don't want to see you move ahead of them.

There are people who don't want to see you out-do them in the church.

There are people who don't want you to be saved in the Lord, who wants to take you to heaven when He comes back again on the clouds of glory.

I Put My Faith in You, O Lord

I put my faith in You, O Lord, that You will give me the strength to get through this day.

I put my faith in You, O Lord, that You will supply all of my needs throughout this day.

I put my faith in You, O Lord, that You will not leave me or forsake me throughout this day.

I put my faith in You, O Lord, that You will answer my prayers.

I put my faith in You, O Lord, that You will keep Your promises to me.

I put my faith in You, O Lord, that You will not allow the devil to tempt me with more than what I can bear.

I put my faith in You, O Lord, that You will be for me and not against me.

I put my faith in You, O Lord, that You will help me to love You and keep Your Commandments.

The Worst Kind Of

The worst kind of demon-possessed people are those who believe they are saved in Jesus when they are really lost in their sins.

The Pharisees were the worst kind of demon-possessed people who believed they were men of God when they were really men of the devil and had Jesus crucified on the cross.

The worst kind of demon-possessed people are those who pretend to be a Christian when they are living in their sins.

They are doing their own will and not doing God's holy will.

The worst kind of demon-possessed people are those who go to church and have no relationship with Jesus Christ.

The worst kind of demon-possessed people are those who compromise God's holy word with the people of the world to please the people of the world.

The worst kind of demon-possessed people are those who know to do right by God's holy word and don't do it.

The worst kind of demon-possessed people are those who go to church and don't love one another.

You and I should not be the worst kind of demon-possessed people who pretend to be a Christian and hold grudges.

You and I should not be the worst kind of demon-possessed people who believe that we are not like the people of the world and are compromising in our faith in Jesus with the people of the world living by the things that they see in this world.

The worst kind of demon-possessed people are those who go to church and have no real, true confession and repentance of their sins unto the Lord Jesus Christ.

You and I should not be the worst kind of demon-possessed people who claim to be like Jesus and will judge and spiritually execute people and condemn them to hell if they are not like you and me who are nothing good without Jesus.

Can be Very Slick and Sly

The devil can be very slick and sly, and so can his human agents.

There are some very slick and sly people who can do something wrong right in front of you and me and we won't see it if we don't have any discernment from the Lord to allow us to see the wrongdoings.

The devil can be very slick and sly and we won't see it if we don't stay prayed-up unto the Lord.

The devil can be very slick and sly and we won't see it if we don't study God's holy word.

The devil has his human agents who are very slick and sly in showing respect of persons.

The devil has his human agents who don't know that they are his human agents doing whatever the devil wants them to do.

No matter how slick and sly the devil and his human agents are, they can't deceive you and me if we love Jesus and keep His Commandments.

The devil can be very slick and sly and his human agents will sooner or later get caught in their slickness and slyness and look bad before anyone who has a relationship with Jesus Christ.

If You Marry Someone Because

If you marry someone because he or she looks good, then sooner or later their imperfections will override their good looks and you will see who they truly are.

If you marry someone because he or she is educated, then sooner or later their imperfections will override their education and you will see who they truly are.

If you marry someone because he or she is good, then sooner or later their imperfections will override their good and you will see who they truly are.

If you marry someone because he or she is helping you, then sooner or later their imperfections will override their helping hands and you will see who they truly are.

If you marry someone because he or she is exciting, then sooner or later their imperfections will override their excitement and you will see who they truly are.

If you marry someone because he or she wants to marry you, then sooner or later their imperfections will override their bond with you and you will see who they truly are.

If you marry someone because he or she rich, then sooner or later their imperfections will override their riches and you will see who they truly are.

If you marry someone for any reason except love, then sooner or later he or she will see your imperfections that will override their trust in you.

If you marry someone for love that is pleasing to the Lord, especially if that someone loves you back

This love will stand the test of time beyond your imperfections, because love covers a multitude of sins.

For a Joke

We should never take someone's soul salvation for a joke.

We should never laugh at people's sins like they're a joke.

We just don't know what our Christian brothers and sisters are going through, but no matter what it is, it's not a joke or a laughing matter.

The devil wants us to take our soul's salvation for a joke.

Nobody can beat the devil laughing at us when we make excuses for sinning against God.

Nobody can beat the devil joking about us if we fall asleep in church.

Nobody can beat the devil joking and laughing at us if we are playing church.

We should never take anyone's soul salvation for a joke.

That's what the devil wants us to do so that we don't care about making any improvements on our Christian walk with Jesus Christ.

Love is a Choice

Love is a choice because you can choose to love people regardless of their flaws.

Love is a choice because you can choose to love people regardless of the mistakes they make.

Love is a choice because you can choose to love your spouse when all infatuation is gone.

Love is a choice because you can choose to love your children even when they are disobedient.

Love is a choice because you can choose to love yourself when you mess things up.

Love is a choice because you can choose to love your enemies who choose not to love you.

Love is a choice because you can choose to love the Lord Jesus Christ who gave you a free will to choose to love Him who gave you that choice that the devil hates.

It's Nothing Compared To

The things that we have in this world are nothing compared to what Jesus will give us when He comes back again to take us to heaven if we are saved in Him.

The spiritual gifts that we have are nothing compared to what Jesus will give us in heaven.

We have dead loved ones who we hope will make it to heaven when Jesus comes back again.

If they make it to heaven, and if we make it to heaven, Jesus will give us His eternal blessings when we get there.

Jesus will give you and me His eternal blessings and bless our loved ones in heaven.

The good deeds we do in this world are nothing compared to what Jesus will give us to do in heaven.

Our life in this world is nothing compared to the eternal life Jesus will give to us in heaven if we are saved in Him.

Only Jesus Can Feel Your

Only Jesus can feel your joy like you feel your joy.

Only Jesus can feel your grief like you feel your grief.

Only Jesus can feel your heartache like you feel your heartache.

Only Jesus can feel your fear like you feel your fear.

Only Jesus can feel your failures like you feel your failures.

Only Jesus can feel your happiness like you feel your happiness.

Only Jesus can feel your achievements like you feel your achievements.

Only Jesus can feel your greatness like you feel your greatness.

Only Jesus can feel your humility like you feel your humility.

When Jesus lived here on earth without sin, He had a perfect heart to feel a lot more things than what you and I can ever feel.

Only Jesus can truly relate to our feelings, whether we feel happy or sad.

Just Because
We are Saved in Jesus Christ

Just because we are saved in Jesus Christ doesn't mean that sin will leave us alone.

Just because we are saved in Jesus Christ doesn't mean that sin will run away from us.

Just because we are saved in Jesus Christ doesn't mean that sin will hide away from us.

Just because we are saved in Jesus Christ doesn't mean that sin will give up on trying to cause us to fall into its deep, dark pits of hell.

Just because we are saved in Jesus Christ doesn't mean that sin will stop stalking us.

Just because we are saved in Jesus Christ doesn't mean that sin will stop calling our name.

Being saved in Jesus Christ gives us the victory over sin.

Being saved in Jesus Christ will crush the head of sin.

Being saved in Jesus Christ gives us the power over sin.

Will Claim to be a Christian

Many people will claim to be a Christian, but will not talk like a Christian.

Many people will claim to be a Christian, but will not dress like a Christian.

Many people will claim to be a Christian, but will not act like a Christian.

Many people will claim to be a Christian, but will not do what a Christian should do.

Many people will claim to be a Christian, but will not live their lives like a Christian.

Being a Christian is being like Jesus every day.

Many people will claim to be a Christian, but will not love everybody.

Many people will claim to be a Christian, but will not love Jesus and keep His Commandments.

Worshipping the Lord

Worshipping the Lord won't depress us.

Worshipping the Lord won't stress us.

Worshipping the Lord won't give us a heartache.

Worshipping the Lord won't disappoint us.

Worshipping the Lord won't discourage us.

Worshipping the Lord won't deceive us.

Worshipping the Lord won't cheat us.

Worshipping the Lord won't hurt us.

Worshipping the Lord won't take anything from us.

Worshipping the Lord won't trick us.

Worshipping the Lord won't enslave us.

Worshipping the Lord won't fail us.

Worshipping the Lord won't make us sick.

Worshipping the Lord won't bring us down.

Worshipping the Lord won't make us insane.

Worshipping the Lord Jesus Christ brings healing.

Worshipping the Lord won't make us liars.

Worshipping the Lord won't kill us.

Worshipping the Lord will give us an abundance of life.

Worshipping the Lord won't give us grief.

Worshipping the Lord won't give us confusion.

Worshipping the Lord won't give us injustice.

Worshipping the Lord won't give us strife.

Worshipping the Lord won't give us envy.

Worshipping the Lord Jesus Christ gives us a peace of mind in this troubled world.

It Will Be Like a Dream Come True

It will be like a dream come true when we see Jesus Christ and all of His angels who will take us to heaven if we are saved in Jesus.

It will be like a dream come true when we see all of our deceased loved ones who Jesus will raise from the grave if they are saved in Him like you and me.

It will be like a dream come true to one day live in heaven where there is nothing but love for everyone and perfect peace throughout the heavens.

It will be like a dream come true when we see God face to face.

We will see our Heavenly Father God, who so loved us that He gave His only begotten Son that whosoever believeth in Him will not perish but will have eternal life.

It will be like a dream come true when we see our only living hope on the clouds of glory with eternal love, eternal joy and eternal life to give to you and me.

It will be like a dream come true beyond all of our worship and obedience and giving God all the glory and praise when we see Jesus Christ shining brighter than the sun.

Jesus will not blind our eyes, because we know what it means to keep our eyes on Jesus today in this dark, sinful world we live in.

It will be like a dream come true for us to live in heaven and talk to Jesus and the angels face to face.

It will be like a dream come true to talk to all of God's prophets of old and talk to all the holy saints who will be in heaven.

It will be like a dream come true for us to visit other worlds and talk to creatures there.

It will be like a dream come true to one day live forever with our Lord and Savior Jesus Christ in the new heaven and new earth that will be beyond all of our prayers in this old sinful world.

It will be like a dream come true that Jesus will give us an immortal body for us to be perfect to have no sins.

It will be like a dream come true that we will leave this old sinful world and not look back on all of our trials we've gone through for us to see our victorious Jesus giving us our stars on our crowns for not denying him before others whose souls belong to Him.

It will be like a dream come true when we overcome this world through the blood of Jesus Christ, who is forevermore real beyond our dreams and will come back again and take us to heaven to live in forever and ever.

It will be like a dream come true to one day see the real Jesus Christ, who is very real beyond the bible scriptures and all of our bible studies that are the truth about Jesus Christ.

It will be like a dream come true to one day live with Jesus in heaven where our spiritual gifts and talents will be clearly seen in the presence of all the angels as well as our good works that will rest so peacefully in heaven.

It will be like a dream come true to one day see a number of holy saints that no one can count except Jesus, who will close all the church doors and stand up and say that it is finished and for us to remain like we are.

It will be like a dream come true to one day have no memories of all our hardships, because Jesus will erase them from our minds while we live in heaven and are evermore free like a bird flying across the sky.

It will be like a dream come true for us to be with Jesus in heaven.

People with good sense want to go to heaven, even if they are living in their sins like there is no tomorrow.

Many people don't believe that there is a God who sent His Son, Jesus Christ, to this world to save us from our sins.

It will be like a dream come true when we aren't tempted by the devil ever again because Jesus will cast the devil and his fallen angels and human agents into the lake of fire and brimstone, while the holy saints will be in the new Jerusalem holy city.

It will be like a dream come true when sin will never exist again while we are in heaven with Jesus Christ.

Anyone who doesn't believe in Jesus and thinks that Jesus isn't real is better off never been born than to have this unrealistic belief.

This is a sign from the Lord for you and me to know that seen and unseen things are real and that God created everything beyond our real-life dreams.

We know that a dream has no substance, like the air we breathe, but every true child of God knows that it will be like a dream come true when we see Jesus on the clouds of glory one day soon.

We don't see the air, but we can feel it and breathe it in and out of our nostrils.

Jesus will fill our dreams with the substance of eternal life when He comes back again to take us to heaven if we are saved in Him.

Why do We Love to Live?

We love to live because we don't want to die and be in the grave where we won't know anything.

We love to live because we don't want to die and be in a grave where we can't see anything.

We love to live because we don't want to die and be in a grave where we can't hear anything.

We love to live because we don't want to die and be in a grave where we can't do anything.

We love to live because we don't want to die and be in a grave where we are not aware of anything.

We love to live because we don't want to die and be in a grave where we can't love anyone.

Why do we love to live?

We love to live because we don't want to die and be in a grave where we can't feel anything.

We love to live because we don't want to die and be in a grave where we can't say anything.

We love to live because we don't want to die and be in a grave where we can't think about anything.

Why do we love to live?

We love to live because we don't want to die and be in a grave where we can't eat any food.

We love to live because we don't want to die and be in a grave where we can't be happy.

We love to live because we don't want to die and be in a grave where we can't achieve anything.

We love to live because we don't want to die and be in a grave where we can't learn anything.

We love to live because we don't want to die and be in a grave where we can't dream about anything.

We love to live because we don't want to die and be in a grave where we can't make any choices.

We love to live because we don't want to die and be in a grave where we can't go to church.

We love to live because we don't want to die and be in a grave where we can't worship the Lord.

We love to live because we don't want to die and be in a grave where we can't praise the Lord.

There are people who don't want to live anymore because of being so depressed.

Why do we love to live when there are people who don't want to live anymore because of being greatly deceived?

Why do we love to live?

We love to live because we don't want to die and be in a grave where we can't take anything with us except our destiny to be in heaven or be in hell.

We love to live because we don't want to die and be in a grave where we can't study the bible.

We love to live because we don't want to die and be in a grave where we can't pray to the Lord.

We love to live because we don't want to die and be in a grave where we can't edify the church.

Why do we love to live?

We love to live because we don't want to die and be in a grave where we can't work out our soul's salvation.

We love to live because we don't want to die and be in a grave where we can't confess and repent of our sins unto the Lord.

We love to live because we don't want to die and be in a grave where we can't deny ourselves and pick up our cross and follow Jesus.

We love to live because we don't want to die and be in a grave where we don't have any more chances to get our hearts, minds and souls all the way right with Jesus.

Why do we love to live?

We love to live because we don't want to die and be in a grave where we can't live again until Jesus Christ comes back again to give us eternal life if we die being saved in Him.

We Christians love to live because we don't want to die and be in the grave where we can't love Jesus Christ and keep His Commandments, even though we are saved in Him while we live today.

We love to live because we don't want to die and be in a grave where we can't have any points of view.

We love to live because we don't want to die and be in a grave where we can't have any opportunities.

We love to live because we don't want to die and be in a grave where we can't have any privileges.

Why do we love to live?

That's something the Lord God can answer so much better than you and me because God gives us life to live with a free will to choose to live for Him or live for the devil before we die.

Why do we love to live?

We love to live because God can prolong our lives for years and years above the grave where we don't want to be, no matter how old we are.

We love to live because we don't want to die and be in a grave where we can't move around or go anywhere.

Why do we love to live?

We love to live because God gives us life for His pleasure and not our own pleasure, which can shorten our lives and cause us to die and be in the grave where we can't be saved if we are lost in our sins.

Most people love to live in this world, no matter how bad things are going on in the world.

Most people love to live, because they don't want to die and be in the grave where no one can do right or do wrong.

Most people love to live, because they don't want to die and be in the grave where no one can live, whether they are good or bad.

Why do we love to live?

We love to live because we believe that life is worth living to give us hope for a better day that is not in the grave where there is no hope for anything.

Why do we love to live?

We people in our right minds love to live because life is great, life is powerful, life is meaningful, life is hope and life is every good thing above the grave that only has one good thing in it, and that is the righteous dead who Jesus will raise up one day and take to heaven when He comes back again.

Why do we love to live?

We love to live because we know that life can surely give everyone something good to look forward to, especially when it comes to living that life unto the Lord Jesus Christ, who should be our main reason why we love to live.

If we love Jesus, we can go to the grave with the assurance of receiving eternal life when Jesus Christ comes back again.

The Greatest Love

We can listen to the greatest love songs and feel the love moving so wonderfully all through our hearts.

We can watch the greatest movies and feel the love moving so majestically all through our souls.

The most loving people on earth are only a glimpse of God's everlasting love.

When we get to heaven, there will be nothing but pure love that we will receive from all the angels.

When we get to heaven, there will be nothing but infinite love that we will receive from other worlds.

When we get to heaven, there will be nothing but perfect love that we will receive from all the saints being a number that no man can count.

You can get the greatest love from your spouse, but that won't even come close to the love you will receive when Jesus comes back again to take you to heaven.

You can get the greatest love from your children, but that won't come close to the love you will receive in heaven.

You can get the greatest love from your friends, but that won't come close to the love you will receive in heaven.

You can get the greatest love from your pets, but that won't come close to the love you will receive in heaven.

There is nothing but pure, everlasting love in heaven where God is love and has greatly extended His love to this fallen, sinful world through His only begotten Son, Jesus Christ, who has redeemed us back to God with His death on the cross to save us from being lost in our sins.

God so loved His Son that He raised Jesus from the grave with power over death that can't enter into heaven where eternal life and God's everlasting love is forevermore inseverable.

The greatest love is what Jesus demonstrated on the cross when He laid down his life for the sins of all the world.

No one can say and believe they are lost because of Jesus not giving them a chance to believe in Him and be saved.

I am So Glad, O Lord

I am so glad, O Lord, that you didn't allow me to be a genius, because I would probably have been full of pride and believed that no one could tell me anything that I didn't already know.

I am so glad, O Lord, that you didn't allow me to be rich, because I would probably have believed I was better than others who were not rich and I would probably have looked down on them like they were nobody.

I am so glad, O Lord, that you didn't allow me to be big, tall and good-looking because I would probably have been having sex with many women and getting some of them pregnant while believing I'm not the father.

I am short, small and of average intelligence man who sometimes struggles with pride, and I believe that if You, O Lord, had allowed me to be a giant of a man I would probably have a mountain of pride like Lucifer and wanted to be god.

I am so glad, O Lord, that you knew what You were doing when you allowed me to not be a giant.

I am so glad, O Lord, that You didn't allow me to have everything, because I would probably have been selfish to the fullest extent and believed that everyone else should pull themselves up by their bootstraps, even though the poor will always be around, just like You said, O Lord.

I am so glad, O Lord, that you didn't allow me to do everything right all the time, because I would probably have been pointing my finger at other people's wrongdoings every day and believing that I was perfect.

Even with all the right that I know today, I still find myself pointing my finger at someone else's wrongdoings, O Lord.

I am so glad, O Lord, that you didn't allow me to be better than anyone else, because I would probably have been comparing myself with those who were less fortunate than me every day, when You, O Lord, didn't create anyone to be a mistake to live in this world where You, O Lord, didn't allow anyone to be lost in their sins without a free will choice.

All that You allowed me to have, O Lord, and all that You allowed me to be, O Lord, is because only You know what is best for me to have, which means I have no reason not to believe in You, O Lord.

I can't speak for anyone else but me, O Lord, because You didn't allow anyone to be lost in their sins without putting Your laws in their hearts so they know some right from wrong and have a conscience — like not eating poison when they know it's poison.

I am so glad, O Lord, that you didn't allow me to destroy myself in my ignorance that tried to make me look so wrong for being alive to have a chance to believe in You, O Lord, and be saved from my ignorant sins.

An Illusion

Someone can believe they are a doctor, when they really are not a doctor — it's just an illusion in their mind.

Someone can believe they have the talent to sing, when he or she can't really sing — it's an illusion in their mind.

Someone can believe they are intelligent, when they are not intelligent — it's just an illusion in their mind.

Some men can believe they are handsome, when they are not handsome — it's just an illusion in their mind.

Some women can believe they are beautiful, when they are not beautiful — it's just an illusion in their mind.

A man can believe he can get any woman he wants, but he can't —it's just an illusion in his mind.

A woman can believe she can get any man she wants, but she can't — it's just an illusion in her mind.

Some men and women can believe they are great, but they aren't great — it's just an illusion in their mind.

Someone can believe they are well, but they are really sick — it's just an illusion in their mind.

Someone can believe they are rich, but they aren't rich — it's just an illusion in their mind.

Someone can believe they are good, but they aren't good — it's just an illusion in their mind.

Someone can believe they can fly a plane, but they aren't a pilot — it's just an illusion in their mind.

Someone can believe they know everything, but they don't know everything — it's just an illusion in their mind.

Someone can believe they are right about what they say, but they aren't right — it's just an illusion in their mind.

Someone can believe they doing the right thing, but they aren't doing the right thing — it's just an illusion in their mind.

Someone in the church can believe they are strong in the Lord, but they aren't strong — it's just an illusion in their mind.

Someone in the church can believe they have no sins, but everyone has sins — it's just an illusion in their mind.

Someone in the church can believe they are filled with the Holy Spirit, but they aren't filled with the Holy Spirit — it's just an illusion in their mind.

Someone in the church can believe they have a relationship with Jesus, but they don't — it's just an illusion in their mind.

Someone in the church can believe they are dressed in modest apparel, but they aren't dressed in modest apparel — it's just an illusion in their mind.

Someone in the church can believe they are a preacher, but God didn't give them the gift to preach — it's just an illusion in their mind.

Someone in the church can believe they love everybody, but they put certain people up on a pedestal — so that equal love is just an illusion in their mind.

Someone in the church can believe they are like Jesus, but they aren't like Jesus — it's just an illusion in their mind.

Illusions are very powerful, but they will never be more powerful than God's holy word that reveals to true reality over every illusion in our minds, in the church and in this world.

Someone can live in an illusion and be happy, they can even die happy in an illusion.

Jesus is real, true happiness for loving Him and keeping His Commandments until we die with the happiness and joy of going to heaven with Jesus when he comes back again on the clouds of glory with all the holy angels.

Sugar and Spice and Everything Nice

Our thoughts will not always be sugar and spice and everything nice.

Our motives will not always be sugar and spice and everything nice.

Our intentions will not always be sugar and spice and everything nice.

Our words will not always be sugar and spice and everything nice.

Our actions will not always be sugar and spice and everything nice.

No one's job will always be sugar and spice and everything nice.

No one's achievements will always be sugar and spice and everything nice.

No one's dreams will always be sugar and spice and everything nice.

No one's education will always be sugar and spice and everything nice.

No one's victories will always be sugar and spice and everything nice.

No one's life will always be sugar and spice and everything nice.

Being a witness of Jesus will not always be sugar and spice and everything nice.

Giving testimonies about what Jesus brought us through will not always be sugar and spice and everything nice.

Denying ourselves and picking up our crosses to follow Jesus will not always be sugar and spice and everything nice.

Loving Jesus and keeping His Commandments will not always be sugar and spice and everything nice.

The Christian journey will not always be sugar and spice and everything nice.

The truth of God's holy word will always be sugar and spice and everything nice to set us free from the devil's lies.

Using our spiritual gifts to build up the church will not always be sugar and spice and everything nice.

Winning souls to Jesus will not always be sugar and spice and everything nice.

Working for Jesus will not always be sugar and spice and everything nice.

Living our lives unto Jesus will not always be sugar and spice and everything nice.

Jesus coming back again will always be sugar and spice and everything nice to you and me and all who will go with Jesus back to heaven one day soon.

Would You Still Love the Lord?

Would you still love the Lord if you couldn't preach anymore sermons about the Lord?

Would you still love the Lord if you couldn't teach anymore bible lessons about the Lord?

Would you still love the Lord if you couldn't sing anymore songs about the Lord?

Would you still love the Lord if you couldn't get well and can't go to church anymore?

Would you still love the Lord if you couldn't hear anymore?

Would you still love the Lord if you couldn't walk anymore?

Would you still love the Lord if you couldn't talk anymore?

Would you still love the Lord if you couldn't drive anymore?

Would you still love the Lord if you couldn't fly a plane anymore?

Would you still love the Lord if you couldn't work anymore?

Would you still love the Lord if you couldn't remember things anymore?

Loving the Lord is deeper than the deepest ocean.

Loving the Lord is higher than the highest mountain.

Would you still love the Lord if you couldn't do anything anymore?

Loving the Lord is purer than the white snowflakes.

Loving the Lord Jesus Christ is forevermore real than our short life spans here on earth where our lives would be so worthless if we didn't love the Lord Jesus Christ.

Everything that we say and do would be so worthless if we didn't love the Lord Jesus Christ.

It would be better for us to have never been born and not exist at all if we don't love Jesus Christ.

If we can't do anything anymore, and if we can't remember anything anymore, loving Jesus is more powerful than anything because if we die loving the Lord Jesus Christ, death can't kill our love and Jesus will raise us from the dead and take us to heaven when He comes back again.

We Don't Know What it's Like

We don't know what it's like to live a hard life if we've always lived in a nice house.

We don't know what it's like to live a hard life if we've always had a nice car to drive.

We don't know what it's like to live a hard life if we've always had clean water to drink.

We don't know what it's like to live a hard life if we've always been in good mental health.

We don't know what it's like to live a hard life if we've always had nice clothes to wear.

We don't know what it's like to live a hard life if we've always been well off.

We don't know what it's like to live a hard life if we've always been treated right.

We don't know what it's like to live a hard life if we've always had good friends.

We don't know what it's like to live a hard life if we've always had it easy.

We don't know what it's like to live a hard life if we've always done everything right.

We don't know what it's like to live a hard life if we've always been in good physical health.

We don't know what it's like to live a hard life if we've always got the victory.

We don't know what it's like to live a hard life if we've always had it good.

We don't know what it's like to live a hard life if we've always had a lot of money.

We don't know what it's like to live a hard life if we've always been sitting down in the church pews and doing nothing for the Lord.

The Free Will Choice

The free will choice is the reason for the great controversy between good and evil in this world.

Up in heaven, Lucifer chose to rebel against God and one third of the angels chose to rebel against God.

Eve chose to eat the fruit from the tree of good, knowledge and evil.

Adam chose to eat the same fruit because Eve gave it to him.

Cain chose to get jealous of his brother, Abel, and killed him because God chose not to accept Cain's offering.

Abel chose to give God an offering that God accepted.

Noah chose to obey God and build an ark.

Noah and his family chose to get in the ark so that God could save them from the flood.

The free will choice is the reason for the great controversy between good and evil.

Ham chose to look upon his father, Noah's, nakedness and he chose not to cover him up.

Abraham chose to obey God and leave his country to go to Canaan.

Abraham chose to obey God to sacrifice his son Isaac as a burnt offering to God.

Lot's wife chose to look back at Sodom and Gomorrah and turned into a pillar of salt.

Joseph's brothers chose to throw him down in the pit and chose to sell Joseph as a slave.

Jacob chose to deceive his father Isaac and made him believe he was Esau, who Isaac wanted to bless.

The free will choice is the reason for the great controversy between good and evil.

Rahab the prostitute chose to hid the Hebrew spies away from the Canaanite soldiers.

Judas chose to betray Jesus for thirty pieces of silver.

Peter chose to deny Jesus three times for the cock to crow.

Jesus chose to leave heaven to come to this sinful world to save us from our sins.

The free will choice is the key to the door of our destinies — will we choose to go with Jesus to heaven when He comes back again or go straight to hell with the devil and his fallen angels?

God has given us a free will to choose, even in our ignorance.

The free will choice is the reason for the great controversy between good and evil in this sinful world.

We can choose to do good or we can choose to do evil.

God will not force us to love Him, who gave us this free will choice to confess and repent of our sins unto his Son, Jesus Christ, and live our lives unto Him or live in our sins unto the devil.

The Truth Points us to Jesus

Telling the truth points us to Jesus, who is the way, the truth and the life.

Believing the truth points us to Jesus, who is the way, the truth and the life.

Living the truth points us to Jesus, who is the way, the truth and the life.

Writing the truth points us to Jesus, who is the way, the truth and the life.

Hearing the truth points us to Jesus, who is the way, the truth and the life.

When has the truth not pointed us to Jesus, who the truth rejoices in?

When has the truth not pointed us to Jesus, who the truth rests its case in?

When has the truth not pointed us to Jesus, who the truth is so free in?

When has the truth not pointed us to Jesus, who the truth is secure in?

When has the truth not pointed us to Jesus, who the truth originates in?

When has the truth not pointed us to Jesus, who the truth is so transparent in?

The truth points us to Jesus, who the truth cannot fail in.

The truth points us to Jesus, who the truth is at its best in.

The truth points us to Jesus, who the truth is very encouraging in.

The truth points us to Jesus, who the truth is beautiful in.

The truth points us to Jesus, who the truth brilliant in.

The truth points us to Jesus, who the truth is also simple in.

The truth points us to Jesus, who the truth is peace in.

The truth points us to Jesus, who the truth is balance in.

The truth points us to Jesus, who the truth is vibrant in.

The truth points us to Jesus, who the truth is humble in.

The truth points us to Jesus, who the truth is good in.

The truth points us to Jesus, who the truth is moral in.

The truth points us to Jesus, who the truth is everlasting in.

The devil and his fallen angels know the truth originates in Jesus, who threw that lying Lucifer and his fallen angels out of heaven.

You Can't Put Your

You can't put your riches and wealth above God's holy law.

You can't put your genius above God's holy law.

You can't put your brilliance above God's holy law.

You can't put your intelligence above God's holy law.

You can't put your common sense above God's holy law.

You can't put your education above God's holy law.

You can't put your husband above God's holy law.

You can't put your wife above God's holy law.

You can't put your children above God's holy law.

You can't put your house above God's holy law.

You can't put your truck above God's holy law.

You can't put your car above God's holy law.

You can't put your airplane above God's holy law.

You can't put your pets above God's holy law.

You can't put your business above God's holy law.

You can't put your job above God's holy law.

You can't put your feelings above God's holy law.

You can't put your logic above God's holy law.

You can't put your theories above God's holy law.

You can't put your opinions above God's holy law.

You can't put your technology above God's holy law.

You can't put your science above God's holy law.

You can't put your wisdom above God's holy law.

You can't put your knowledge above God's holy law.

You can't put your clothes above God's holy law.

You can't put your jewelry above God's holy law.

You can't put your friends above God's holy law.

You can't put your comings and goings above God's holy law.

You can't put your achievements above God's holy law.

You can't put your food above God's holy law.

You can't put your talent above God's holy law.

You can't put your skills above God's holy law.

You can't put your yourself above God's holy law.

God's holy law is perfect.

God's holy law is righteous.

God's holy law is good.

God's holy law is God's character.

You and I can't put anything above God's holy law.

God' holy law will stand forever and ever.

Jesus says, "If you love Me, you will keep My Commandments," which is God's holy law for all the world to keep.

God will never change His holy law, even though rebellious people will try to change it because they want to be above God's holy law.

While They are Still Alive

Talk nice to people while they are still alive, because after they are dead and gone to the grave it's too late to talk nice to them.

Treat people right while they are still alive, because after they are dead and gone to the grave it's too late to treat them right.

Tell people the truth while they are still alive, because after they are dead and gone to the grave it's too late to tell them the truth.

Be happy for people while they are still alive, because after they are dead and gone to the grave it's too late to be happy for them.

Respect people while they are still alive, because after they are dead and gone to the grave it's too late to respect to them.

Forgive people while they are still alive, because after they are dead and gone to the grave it's too late for them to know they are forgiven.

Help people while they are still alive, because after they are dead and gone to the grave it's too late to help them.

Pray for people while they are still alive, because after they are dead and gone to the grave it's too late to pray for them.

Love people while they are still alive, because after they are dead and gone to the grave it's too late to love them.

Encourage people while they are still alive, because after they are dead and gone to the grave it's too late to encourage them.

Be fair to people while they are still alive, because after they are dead and gone to the grave it's too late to be fair to them.

Spread the good news about Jesus Christ to people while they are still alive, because after they are dead and gone to the grave it's too late to spread the good news about Jesus Christ to them.

Live right unto the Lord Jesus before people while they are still alive, because after they are dead and gone to the grave it's too late to live right unto the Lord Jesus before them.

A Christian and a Worldly Person

A Christian and a worldly person are so different from one another.

A Christian believes in Jesus Christ and a worldly person doesn't believe in Jesus Christ.

A Christian will pray to Jesus and ask Jesus to help them through the hardships they have in their lives.

A worldly person will try to get through the hardships on their own strength, which is no strength compared to Jesus.

A Christian and a worldly person are so different from one another.

A Christian loves Jesus and keeps His Commandments.

A worldly person loves this world and breaks Jesus' Commandments.

A Christian will pray to Jesus and ask Jesus to work out the problems in his or her life.

A worldly person will not pray to Jesus and ask Him to work out the problems in his or her life.

A worldly person will try to work out his or her problems using their own intellect.

A Christian and a worldly person are so different from one another.

A Christian lives in the light of truth about Jesus.

A worldly person lives in the darkness of the devil's lies.

A Christian will trust Jesus and wait on Jesus, who is always on time to answer prayers.

A worldly person will trust this world to give them whatever they want and they will be in a hurry to get it.

This world is not always on time to be there for anyone, but Jesus is always on time to be there for us as long as we trust Him and wait on Him and don't try to get ahead of Him, which is something we can never do.

Is a Lot to Live For

A loving and faithful spouse is a lot to live for.

Obedient children are a lot to live for.

Loving parents are a lot to live for.

Making achievements is a lot to live for.

Being wise is a lot to live for.

Loving everybody is a lot to live for.

Being humble is a lot to live for.

Doing better in life is a lot to live for.

Working is a lot to live for.

Justice is a lot to live for.

Equality is a lot to live for.

Giving a helping hand is a lot to live for.

Saving lives is a lot to live for.

Prosperity is a lot to live for.

Good mental and physical health is a lot to live for.

Peace is a lot to live for.

Knowing the truth is a lot to live for.

Freedom is a lot to live for.

Unity is a lot to live for.

Communication is a lot to live for.

Being protected is a lot to live for.

Having faith in Jesus is more than a lot to live for.

Loving Jesus and keeping His Commandments is more than a lot to live for.

Being saved in Jesus is more than a lot to live for.

Working for Jesus is more than a lot to live for.

Being Lost in Sin

Being lost in sin is like being lost in our mind.

Being lost in sin is like being lost in the forest.

Being lost in sin is like being lost out in the ocean.

Being lost in sin is like losing everything we have.

Being lost in sin is like being lost in the outer space.

Being lost in sin is like losing our memory.

Being lost in sin is like losing our dignity.

Being lost in sin is like being lost on the highway road.

Being lost in sin is like being lost in the night.

Being lost in sin is like being lost in another city.

There is nothing good about being lost in sin.

Being lost in sin is like losing you high-paying job.

Being lost in sin is like being lost for the right words to say.

Being lost in sin is like losing our life for doing something bad.

Jesus knows how bad it is if we are lost in our sins that He died on the cross and rose from the grave to save us from.

Being lost in sin is like losing a baby.

If we believe in Jesus Christ, He will save us from being lost in our sins.

Being lost in sin is like losing a dear friend.

Being lost in sin is like losing our loved ones.

Being lost in sin is like being lost in oneself for not choosing to confess and repent of our sins, be baptized and live for Jesus Christ, because no one can ever be lost in Jesus Christ.

All About Winning Souls

Sermons are all about winning souls to the Lord.

Bible school lessons are all about winning souls to the Lord.

Gospel songs are all about winning souls to the Lord.

Inspirational poetry is all about winning souls to the Lord.

Testimonies are all about winning souls to the Lord.

Being humble is all about winning souls to the Lord.

Being content is all about winning souls to the Lord.

Being joyful is all about winning souls to the Lord.

Being truthful is all about winning souls to the Lord.

Being loving is all about winning souls to the Lord.

Being friendly is all about winning souls to the Lord.

Being compassionate is all about winning souls to the Lord.

Being giving is all about winning souls to the Lord.

Being helpful is all about winning souls to the Lord.

Being gentle is all about winning souls to the Lord.

Having temperance is all about winning souls to the Lord.

Being faithful is all about winning souls to the Lord.

Being kind is all about winning souls to the Lord.

Being strong is all about winning souls to the Lord.

Being forgiving is all about winning souls to the Lord.

Being encouraging is all about winning souls to the Lord.

Being thoughtful is all about winning souls to the Lord.

Being thankful is all about winning souls to the Lord.

Being wise is all about winning souls to the Lord.

Being respectful is all about winning souls to the Lord.

Being brave is all about winning souls to the Lord.

Being good is all about winning souls to the Lord.

Our spiritual gifts are all about winning souls to the Lord.

Our prayers are all about winning souls to the Lord.

Our works are all about winning souls to the Lord.

Our Christian life is all about winning souls to our Lord and Savior Jesus Christ, who is all about saving every soul from being lost in sin, even if everybody doesn't believe in Jesus to be saved.

Your Holy Spirit, O Lord

There was a time in my life when I wasn't a Christian and I had some demons in me.

Those demons controlled my life and caused me to feel so hopeless.

When I wasn't a Christian, the Lord was so good to me to bring me this far in His goodness for me to confess and repent of my sins and give my heart to Him.

You gave me Your Holy Spirit, O Lord, for me to love You and love my spiritual brothers and sisters in the church, as well as everybody else.

Your Holy Spirit, O Lord, causes me to feel very sorrowful about living in rebellion against You many years ago.

Your Holy Spirit, O Lord, brings tears to my eyes when I feel the power of Your Holy Spirit, O Lord, in the prayers and in some of my spiritual brothers and sisters.

It makes my heart glad to know that I have spiritual brothers and sisters who love You, O Lord.

I need your Holy Spirit, O Lord, to live in me who would die so fragile and hopeless without You, O Lord, in my life.

Your Holy Spirit, O Lord, shows me the truth about myself and the truth about others who need Your Holy Spirit, O Lord, to help them to live right unto You.

Your Holy Spirit, O Lord, nurtures my broken mind and feeds it with Your holy word to strengthen my mind to think on You, O Lord, who is the great healer of broken minds and broken hearts.

Your Holy Spirit, O Lord, takes my broken prayers up to You and Your Holy Spirit will fix my broken prayers so they are suitable for You, O Lord, to answer them.

Without Your Holy Spirit in my life, I am better off never being born just like Judas was better off never being born for betraying You, my Lord and Savior Jesus Christ.

More Worth than Wealth

A good name is more worth than wealth.

Good health is more worth than wealth.

Love is more worth than wealth.

A peace of mind is more worth than wealth.

Joy is more worth than wealth.

The truth is more worth than wealth.

Freedom is more worth than wealth.

Justice is more worth than wealth.

Faith in Jesus is more worth than wealth.

Worshipping Jesus is more worth than wealth.

Hope in Jesus is more worth than wealth.

Keeping Jesus' Commandments is more worth than wealth.

Being saved in Jesus is more worth than wealth.

Wealth can come and wealth can go, but Jesus is eternal and fills up the heavens with everlasting wealth forever beyond worldly wealth that is not worth a penny to God.

We Can Believe That We

We can believe that we gave up a job we loved, when the Lord has something much better in store for us.

We can believe we are not making any improvements in our lives, but the Lord can open a door of opportunity to bless our lives.

We can believe that nothing great will happen in our lives, but the Lord can surprise us with great things in our lives.

We can believe that we have failed in our life, but the Lord can give us the victory over our past mistakes.

We can believe that we are not going anywhere in our lives, but the Lord can take us very far, especially on our Christian journey.

We can believe we messed up real bad in our lives, but the Lord can make things good in our lives for living our lives unto Him.

We can believe we missed out on a lot of things in life, but the Lord can give us a lot of His blessings for returning faithful tithes and offerings unto Him.

We can believe we are not smart, but the Lord can sharpen our minds and expand our minds with the wisdom and knowledge of His holy word for us to make the right choices in our lives.

We can believe we are not reaching out to a lot of lost souls, but the Lord can bless our spiritual gifts to reach around the world to places we've never been

We can believe the Lord is finished with us, but the Lord can give us more work to do for Him.

The Bible is a True Storybook

The bible is a true storybook about real people who lived over a thousand years ago.

The bible is a true storybook about good and evil people who lived in this world together.

Many people today love to read imaginary books and will get deep into the stories like they are real.

We can read the bible and get deep into it because the bible is a real, true storybook that can surely change our lives for the better if we read it.

There are imaginary stories that are powerful and cause us to believe they are true, but the bible is filled with true stories about real people who were good and evil.

The good holy people worshipped the real, true, living God and the evil people worshipped false gods.

The bible is a true storybook that has been passed down through the centuries.

No evilness could weaken the bible's bright light of God's love, mercy, truth and grace in this dark, sinful world where the imaginary is rampant.

The bible is a true storybook about a real, true, living God who sent His Son, Jesus Christ, to this world where many people believe in imaginary gods that can't answer their prayers and can't heal their sin-sick souls.

Many people love to read imaginary books and will live their lives by them, as if they're real.

The bible is a real storybook that we can truly live by because Jesus Christ is real and has fulfilled every story in the bible to point to Him who gave up His life on the cross to die for the sins of all the world as

Jesus rose from the grave with victory over death to give us eternal life in the end.

The bible is a true storybook that we can truly believe to correct us and encourage us to live right by a true, living God that no imaginary story could ever out-shine in this dark world where the bible is a lamp unto my feet and a light unto my path.

The bible is also a true storybook about a real, true devil who is running to and fro throughout the earth trying to devour whoever he can so they are lost in their sins and go to hell with him in the end.

It Pleases the Lord

It pleases the Lord for especially every child of God to love one another all the same.

It pleases the Lord for us to accept one another for who we are, as we are all different from one another.

It pleases the Lord for us to not be opinionated about one another who the Lord truly knows inside and outside the church.

It pleases the Lord for you and me to not judge one another, because only the Lord knows our whole hearts day after day and night after night.

It pleases the Lord for you and me to not think highly of ourselves and believe we are better than others who are not as smart as we are.

It pleases the Lord for us to humble ourselves before Him and before one another to be like Him who humbled Himself when He lived in this proud, sinful world.

It pleases the Lord for you and me to rejoice with one another when things are going really well in our lives.

It pleases the Lord for you and me to grieve with one another when we lose our loved ones in our families.

It pleases the Lord for His church body of believers in Him to be of one accord in spreading the good news about Him to all the world.

It pleases the Lord for you and me to not cause one another to stumble or fall away from Him who is for us all to be saved in Him, whether we are rich or poor, educated or not educated.

It pleases the Lord for you and me to speak the truth in love and live the truth that is all about Him who is the faithful and true Lord and Savior of the world.

It pleases the Lord Jesus Christ for us to pray for one another, encourage one another and help one another hold onto Him through our trials that are not easy for us to bear.

Want to Play God

Many people want to play God by using advanced technology as a substitute for the human race.

Many people want to play God by using medical technology that can't perform a miracle to save a life like God can.

Many people want to play God and use sports to captivate an audience of thousands of people who cheer for talented men and women who have no heaven to put them in like God does.

Many people want to play God on the TV screen and in the movie theaters, but they can never move hearts to repent like God's goodness can.

Many people want to play God in politics by making promises to people, but only God's promises will always stand.

Many people want to play God in the workplace where people get paychecks and can spend it all up, but only God will open the windows of heaven and pour out blessings upon people who will have no room to receive it all from God for returning faithful tithes and offerings to God.

Many people want to play God with their education and wealth because they believe they are self-made, but it was God who allowed them to get a good education and accumulate wealth that will never rise above God.

Many people want to play God in the church where they believe they know it all and see no need to learn anything good from you and me, even though God listens to our prayers and doesn't believe He is too good to not answer them in His perfect, eternal heaven.

It's Because of Jesus

It's because of Jesus that the fallen angles can't rule this world.

Fallen angels from heaven are spiritual beings we can't see who are our enemies.

If the fallen angels could rule this world, there would be nothing but evil everywhere.

You and I and every human being would be doing evil things all the time.

There would be nothing good about any human being here on earth.

It's because of Jesus Christ that this world still exists with life that the fallen angels hate to see.

They hate to see you and me live our life unto Jesus day by day.

If Jesus had not gone to war against Lucifer up in heaven, then heaven would be filled with evil angels following Lucifer.

Instead, Lucifer is the devil on earth today with his fallen angels who have failed to rule this world because of Jesus Christ.

Jesus defeated Lucifer and all of his fallen angels up in heaven and Jesus defeated Lucifer the devil and all of his fallen angels here on earth.

Our real, true enemies are spiritual beings who fell from heaven because of their rebellion against God, who so loved the world that He gave us His only begotten Son that whosoever believeth in Him will not perish but shall have eternal life.

If Jesus had not given up His life on the cross to save us from our sins, then risen from the grave, the devil and all of his fallen angels would have destroyed this world thousands of years ago.

All the evil spiritual beings would have caused every human being to turn against each other and kill each other, with all the animals and other creatures joining in on the kill.

It's because of Jesus that the devil and his fallen angels could never rule this world and cause every human being to be lost in sin.

What good would our free will choices be to us if the devil could rule this world?

Jesus did not allow that and He redeemed us back to God.

If I Never

If everything was good in my life, I would believe that I don't' need You, my Lord.

If I never say anything wrong, I would believe that I don't need You, my Lord.

If I never do anything wrong, I would believe that I don't need You, my Lord.

If I never make any mistakes, I would believe that I don't need You, my Lord.

If I never make any bad choices, I would believe that I don't need You, my Lord.

If I knew all things, I would believe that I don't need You, my Lord.

If I could see all things, I would believe that I don't need You, my Lord.

If I could do all things, I would believe that I don't need You, my Lord.

If I never had any hardships, I would believe that I don't need You, my Lord.

I know that I can only speak for myself, because there are many people who don't believe they need You, O Lord, because they are very rich and believe they have no need of You who can take away their riches and wealth.

The angels in heaven are perfect, but they still need You, my Lord and Savior Jesus Christ who created them perfect with a free will to love and obey you forever and ever.

O Lord, You created Adam and Eve perfect, but they stopped believing they needed to always worship you because they desired a fruit that caused them to give the devil dominion over this world.

If everything was perfect in my life, I would believe that I don't need You, my Lord, because I would be like Adam who sinned against You because he believed he was right in his own eyes to eat that fruit.

The Spiritual Life

The spiritual life is truly all about living our lives unto Jesus Christ.

Many people will talk about living a spiritual life that is at its best in Jesus Christ.

The spiritual life is the best life to live, but it can only be lived in Jesus Christ.

There is no higher spiritual life to live above Jesus Christ, who was the highest spirit in heaven next to God, His heavenly Father, who sent Jesus to this world in flesh and bone to relate to the human race and bring us back to God.

No one can give any good, lasting spiritual advice to anyone if it's not about loving and obeying Jesus Christ.

The bible is the best spiritual book to read and live by because the bible points us to the spiritual life that Jesus lived without sin when He lived here on earth.

The greatest spiritual life to live is to live our lives unto Jesus Christ, who is higher than all the spiritual angels in heaven.

The spiritual life is mostly unseen all around you and me every day.

We can't see God and the angels, who are not made of flesh and bone like you and me.

The spiritual life is truly all about living our lives unto the Lord Jesus Christ because there is no other spiritual life to live that can heal a broken spirit better than Jesus.

When Jesus heals us, we are truly healed.

No other spiritual life can do this.

It makes the spiritual fallen angels tremble because they know that the spiritual life is truly all about living our lives giving Jesus all the glory and praise for creating us with a body and spirit to live a spiritual life unto Jesus Christ.

We Can Shed All of Our Tears

We can shed all of our tears unto the Lord, who knows all of our sad feelings and will truly comfort us.

If we shed our tears unto the Lord, we can get them all out and have none left to shed.

We can shed all of our tears unto the Lord who will make us feel so much better after the last teardrop falls.

Only the Lord always knows how we truly feel about the death of our loved ones as the tears drop from our eyes.

Jesus knows what it's like to shed some tears, because Jesus wept at the death of Lazarus who Jesus loved.

Even if we see someone else shedding some tears, it will cause us to feel sad if we have a heart full of compassion.

We can cry really hard, and only the Lord Jesus Christ will truly understand, while many people can be judgmental and believe you and I must have treated our loved ones bad when they were alive.

If we hold back our tears, we are truly hurting ourselves and we won't grow stronger as human beings who God created with feelings.

Many men believe they aren't supposed to cry, but no man can ever be more of a man than Jesus, who wept with tears falling from His eyes.

When we cry, we can always get it all out with Jesus, who will truly understand our loud crying.

We can give that pain to Jesus because no one else can comfort us better than our Lord Jesus Christ.

We can always shed all of our tears unto the Lord Jesus Christ, who always knows how to dry up our tears and make us feel so much better, as if we never broke down in sadness or shed any tears.

Will Use the Bible Scriptures

Many people will use the bible scriptures to control others.

Many people will use the bible scriptures to benefit themselves.

Many people will use the bible scriptures to make people look bad.

Many people will use the bible scriptures to correct people in their wrongdoings but not correct their own wrongdoings.

Many people will use the bible scriptures to make themselves look right when they're doing something wrong.

Many people will use the bible scriptures in the wrong way to deceive others.

Many people will use the bible scriptures to put people in bondage.

Many people will use the bible scriptures for their own selfish reasons.

Many people will use the bible scriptures in the wrong way to do evil.

There is no lie in the bible, but liars will make it look like a lie with their evolution theories.

There is no lie in the bible, but liars will misinterpret it to suit their ways of living.

There is no lie in the bible, but liars don't believe this to be true.

There is no lie in the bible, but liars don't want to live right by the bible.

Many church folks will use the bible scriptures to cover up their own true character so they can be like a wolf in sheep's clothing.

This would be you and me if we are only pretending to love Jesus by only going through the motions with no true conversion in our hearts.

I Thank You, O Lord

I thank You, O Lord, for looking down on me from up in Your heavens on high.

I thank You, O Lord, for spending some time with me, who is nowhere near to Your all-knowing mind and all-seeing eyes.

O Lord God, You sent Your only begotten Son, Jesus Christ, to this sinful world to save me from my sins as if I was the only sinner living among billions of other perfect people in this world.

O Lord, my God, you know all of my heart that I will never know like You, who always knows how to make me feel so loved by You.

I thank You, O Lord, for taking the time to talk to me and listen to me who you see to be Your child who is longing for Your Holy Spirit to live in me day after day.

O my Lord God, You are all present and all around me day after day.

I see You in good Christian people, in nature and most of all I see You, my Lord God, in Your holy word that is filled with nothing but the truth about You.

O my Lord God, I thank you for looking down on poor little me who You want to be in heaven with You when You send Your Son, Jesus Christ, back to this world again to take me to heaven as if I was the only one here on earth.

I thank you, O Lord, for looking down on me from heaven and giving me Your extended time for me to truly know that it's You who kept me alive to see this day that I have no excuse to not love You and keep Your Commandments.

O Lord, You have brushed off my ignorance through Your holy word that is all truth about You for me to live my life unto You with my conscience awakened in making You my choice every day, O my Lord God.

Life Goes on Beyond

Life goes on beyond what we said wrong.

Life goes on beyond what we did wrong.

Life goes on beyond what we didn't say that was right to say.

Life goes on beyond what we didn't do that was right to do.

Life goes on beyond the mistakes we made.

Life goes on beyond what we messed up.

Life goes on beyond what we can't do.

Life goes on beyond what we don't have.

Life goes on beyond what we didn't know yesterday.

Life goes on beyond what we don't know today.

Life goes on beyond where we didn't go to.

Life goes on beyond what we got and didn't want.

Life goes on beyond our dream that didn't come true.

Life goes on beyond what we didn't achieve.

Life goes on beyond our misfortunes.

Life goes on beyond our past.

Life goes on beyond everything we did wrong.

Life goes on beyond every word we said wrong.

Life goes on beyond that old sinful creature being made a new spiritual creature in Jesus Christ.

Life goes on beyond that old carnal-minded man, woman boy and girl having a new spiritual mind in Jesus Christ.

Life goes on beyond this old sinful world that will one day pass away in fire and brimstone beneath eternal life in heaven where life will go on in Jesus Christ.

This Whole World is Vulnerable

This whole world is vulnerable to not knowing what a day will bring.

This whole world is vulnerable to suffering and pain.

This whole world is vulnerable to crimes.

This whole world is vulnerable to disappointments.

This whole world is vulnerable to heartaches.

This whole world is vulnerable to grief.

This whole world is vulnerable to flaws.

This whole world is vulnerable to mistakes.

This whole world is vulnerable to accidents.

This whole world is vulnerable to war.

This whole world is vulnerable to evil.

This whole world is vulnerable to conspiracy.

This whole world is vulnerable to the unpredictable.

This whole world is vulnerable to diseases.

This whole world is vulnerable to viruses.

This whole world is vulnerable to corruption.

This whole world is vulnerable to deception.

This whole world is vulnerable to one-world order.

This whole world is vulnerable to destruction.

This whole world is vulnerable to violence.

This whole world is vulnerable to selfishness.

This whole world is vulnerable to natural disasters.

This whole world is vulnerable to troubled times.

This whole world is vulnerable to immorality.

This whole world is vulnerable to sin.

This whole world is vulnerable to death.

Jesus Christ foreknew that this whole world would be vulnerable to hell when Adam and Eve were cast out of the Garden of Eden for disobeying God.

Beyond this very vulnerable world, Jesus gave up His life on the cross to save us from being lost in our sins and He rose from the grave to give us eternal life.

When Jesus lived here on earth without sin, He overcame this vulnerable world to give you and me the power to overcome this vulnerable world of sin for believing in Him to be saved.

If we are saved, we aren't vulnerable and we can never weaken and break into pieces because Jesus is forever stronger than this vulnerable world that is weak in love that is strong in every real, true Christian.

Real, true Christians love Jesus and their neighbors, who are everyone in this whole vulnerable world.

Setting the Stage for One-World Order

The increase in political strife is setting the stage for one-world order.

The increase of government shutdowns is setting the stage for one-world order.

The increase in wars is setting the stage for one-world order.

The increase in lawlessness is setting the stage for one-world order.

The increase in crimes is setting the stage for one-world order.

The increase in terrorists is setting the stage for one-world order.

The increase in sexual immorality is setting the stage for one-world order.

The increase in spiritualism is setting the stage for one-world order.

The increase in drug abuse is setting the stage for one-world order.

The increase in knowledge is setting the stage for one-world order.

The increase in fame is setting the stage for one-world order.

The increase in living in pleasure is setting the stage for one-world order.

The increase in technology is setting the stage for one-world order.

The increase in prosperity is setting the stage for one-world order.

The increase in millionaires and billionaires is setting the stage for one-world order.

The increase in poverty is setting the stage for one-world order.

The increase in inflation is setting the stage for one-world order.

The increase in pollution is setting the stage for one-world order.

The increase in climate change is setting the stage for one-world order.

The increase in social media is setting the stage for one-world order.

The increase in bad news broadcasting is setting the stage for one-world order.

The increase in earthquakes is setting the stage for one-world order.

The increase in hurricanes is setting the stage for one-world order.

The increase in tornadoes is setting the stage for one-world order.

The increase in wildfires is setting the stage for one-world order.

The increase in floods is setting the stage for one-world order.

The increase in heatwaves is setting the stage for one-world order.

The increase in snow blizzards is setting the stage for one-world order.

The increase in mudslides is setting the stage for one-world order.

The increase in sinkholes is setting the stage for one-world order.

The increase in droughts is setting the stage for one-world order.

The increase in famines is setting the stage for one-world order.

The increase in diseases is setting the stage for one-world order.

The increase in viruses is setting the stage for one-world order.

The increase in starvation is setting the stage for one-world order.

The increase in homelessness is setting the stage for one-world order.

The increase in selfishness is setting the stage for one-world order.

The increase in religious rivalry is setting the stage for one-world order.

The increase in falling away from the church is setting the stage for one-world order.

The increase in evolution beliefs is setting the stage for one-world order.

The increase in rebelling against God is setting the stage for one-world order.

The increase in rejecting Jesus Christ is setting the stage for one-world order.

The increase in breaking God's Commandments is setting the stage for one-world order.

The increase in blaspheming the Holy Spirit is setting the stage for one-world order.

The increase in misinterpreting God's holy word is setting the stage for one-world order.

The increase in living in sin is setting the stage for one-world order.

The one-world order will surely not be about God setting up His kingdom on earth.

The one-world order will not be about the real Jesus Christ, who will not be seen walking around from place to place in this world.

Every eye will see the real Jesus Christ up in the sky.

The one-world order will be about the devil giving his power to the pope to rule this whole world that won't last long because the real Jesus Christ will come back again and cause all the devil's human agents to drop dead from the brightness of His eternal shining light that only the living righteous people can look upon and live to be changed from mortal to immortality.

Also in the Simple Things in Life

Regardless of theologies, Jesus is also in the simple things in life.

Regardless of philosophies, Jesus is also in the simple things in life.

Regardless of religions, Jesus is also in the simple things in life.

Regardless of technologies, Jesus is also in the simple things in life.

Regardless of mysteries, Jesus is also in the simple things in life.

Regardless of education, Jesus is also in the simple things in life.

Regardless of educated guesses, Jesus is also in the simple things in life.

Regardless of phenomenons, Jesus is also in the simple things in life.

Regardless of great wisdom, Jesus is also in the simple things in life.

Regardless of miracles, Jesus is also in the simple things in life.

A simple thing in life can be a smile that Jesus is also in.

A simple thing in life can be a helping hand that Jesus is also in.

A simple thing in life can be being honest that Jesus is also in.

A simple thing in life can be a listening ear that Jesus is also in.

A simple thing in life can be not making the same mistakes that Jesus is also in.

Jesus is also in the simple things in life, regardless of intellectual words.

Jesus is also in the simple things in life, regardless of sophisticated ministries in the church.

A simple thing in life can be giving encouragement that Jesus is also in.

A simple thing in life can be laughter that Jesus is also in.

A simple thing in life can be getting a good night's sleep that Jesus is also in.

Regardless of the complicated things in life, Jesus is also in the simple things in life.

A simple thing in life can be taking good care of yourself that Jesus is also in.

A simple thing in life is being in control of yourself that Jesus is also in.

A simple thing in life is treating people right that Jesus is also in.

A simple thing in life is not forming your own opinion about anyone who only Jesus knows completely.

When Jesus Lived on Earth

When Jesus lived on earth without sin among the people back in the bible days, He knew everything about the future.

Jesus knew everything about what's in this world today, but He didn't speak to the people about it.

If Jesus had talked to the people about airplanes, trucks and cars, the people would not have understood him.

They would've probably believed that Jesus had lost His mind.

When Jesus lived on earth without sin among the people back in the bible days, He knew everything about today's technology and science but He didn't speak about that to the people then because He knew they would not understand him.

The people back in the bible days just didn't realize they were in the presence of a God who knew all the past, all the present and all the future that was and is all about Jesus being in control of all things.

The people back in the bible days didn't know they were in the presence of a God who knew all about the heavens and all about other worlds that He created.

We are no better off than the people back in the bible days because with all of our technology and science today, Jesus is still forevermore advanced in all things that He can do and has done up in heaven and in other worlds.

Jesus is far more advanced in the things we can't see.

When Jesus lived on earth without sin among people who were born in sin, they didn't know they were in the presence of eternal life because it was covered over in flesh and bone to be nailed to the cross and shed blood for the sins of all the world.

We are no better off than the people back in the bible days because we can live our lives like there is no eternal life in Jesus Christ, who we can nail on the cross all over again with disbelief in Him that causes us to live by eyesight and not by faith in Jesus.

If There was No God

What is the use in existing in this world today if there is no God?

What is the use in having a soul if there is no God?

What is the use in going to church if there is no God?

What is the use in having eyes to see if there is no God?

What is the use in having ears to hear if there is no God?

What is the use in having a mind to think if there is no God?

What is the use in having a heart to feel if there is no God?

What is the use in having a tongue to talk if there is no God?

What is the use in having a body if there is no God?

What is the use in having faith in Jesus Christ if there is no God?

What is the use in living if there is no God?

We wouldn't exist at all if there is no God.

Nothing would exist if there is no God.

Only a fool would believe there is no God.

A fool will believe that he or she exists and won't go around saying otherwise.

A fool knows that he or she was born out of their mother's womb to exist in this world, but that same fool will believe there is no God, who is the beginning of all existence.

There would be no theories, opinions and no educated guesses if there is no God.

There would be no worlds, no stars and no outer space if there is no God.

There would be no free will choice for anyone to choose to be a fool if there is no God.

Lucifer would never have existed to rebel against God if there is no God.

There would be no you and me if there is no God.

God is the origin of all life, so only a fool would believe there is no god.

Death knows there is a God because death can convince a fool that there is a God who can spare a fool's life from the shadows of death.

Because of Sin

Because of sin, everyone has some kind of mental defect.

Some people have more mental defects than other people.

Because of sin, the richest man and woman can say something foolish and do something foolish.

Because of sin, the most genius man and woman can say something foolish and do something foolish.

Lucifer had a mental defect and believed he could take God's place on His holy throne up in heaven; instead, he was cast out for rebelling against God.

Lucifer caused his own mental defect because he wanted to be God when that was impossible, because God created him.

Because of sin, everyone won't think right all the time.

Because of sin, everyone won't say the right words all the time.

Because of sin, everyone won't do right all the time.

The holiest of men and women will fall short of the glory of God because of having a sinful nature that causes them to sin against God in some kind of seen and unseen way.

Jesus Christ, our Lord and Savior, foreknew that because of sin being in this world He would have to give up His sinless life and die on the cross for our sins and rise from the grave with victory over death.

The blood Jesus shed will cleanse us of our sins if we confess and repent of our sins.

Because of sin, everyone has a flaw to be recognized.

Because of sin, the righteous and the wicked go to the grave, but the righteous dead are saved in Jesus Christ.

Jesus will come back again to raise the righteous dead and give eternal life to the righteous saints, whether they were knowledgeable or not so knowledgeable of God's holy word.

We Can't Always Be

We can't always be right about someone and we can't always be wrong about someone, because our senses can deceive us and make us believe something that is not true.

The devil is very powerful and can cause us to believe someone is telling a lie when they are actually telling the truth.

We can be deceived and not see the truth about someone.

Someone can be good, but we can believe that he or she is bad.

Someone can be bad, but we can believe that he or she is good.

We can't always be right about someone and we can't always be wrong about someone who we don't truly know.

We can assume that we know someone, even though we don't hang around with them.

We can't always know someone or how he or she behaves, especially on the spur of the moment.

You and I don't know how we will behave ourselves when we're under pressure.

We can be so right about someone and we can be so wrong about someone, even if we have known that person for a long time.

Only the Lord always knows everyone's heart, even when their actions can be questioned and we don't know if they're being truthful with us.

We may think that someone is trying to hurt someone else, when they might just be defending themselves.

You and I don't know everything and we can't judge anyone or assume what's in their minds and hearts.

People's actions won't always appear to be what they are, and we can't assume things about someone when we have no real proof.

Only Jesus will always have proof about you and me and everyone else, and He will know whether we are loving Him and keeping His Commandments.

Only Jesus will always have proof about who will be saved in Him and make it to heaven when He comes back again.

Prayers from Our Hearts

Prayers from our hearts will cheer God's heart, no matter if our prayers are long or short.

God loves to listen to prayers from our hearts, but prayers with long words from our heads are empty to God, no matter how good our prayers sound to others.

We can't impress God with long prayers if they are not from our hearts.

The Pharisees prayed long prayers to God out in public, where they could be seen by people, but their prayers were empty to God because they were not from their hearts.

It's not wrong for us to pray long prayers to God, who loves for us to pray to Him from our hearts and not from our heads.

God is not impressed with our long, dressed up prayers if they are not from our hearts.

God would answer a simple little child's prayer if it was from his or her heart, and God will answer an uneducated man or woman's prayer if it's from their hearts.

God will answer long and short prayers if they are from our hearts and not from our heads.

A prayer from our heads will cause God to frown at us because God wants us to be real with Him from our hearts.

Prayers from our hearts will surely get God's attention, but prayers from our heads are so worthless to God.

God loves to listen to and answer long prayers from our hearts, and God loves to listen to and answer short prayers from our hearts.

Prayers from our heads, whether they are long or short, are so empty to God.

If our prayers are from our hearts, the Holy Spirit can work with us to take our prayers up to God, who is not interested in prayers from the head like the Pharisees loved to pray.

They believed that God would hear their heartless prayers and answer them, even though they rejected Jesus Christ, who is the Word of God and the heart of God.

Prayers from our hearts will move God's heart for God to answer our prayers on His time, no matter if our prayers are long or short.

There were times when Jesus prayed to God all night long from His heart and God never got tired of listening to Jesus, who is His only begotten Son that God sent to this world to save us from our sins.

Pray Without Ceasing

The Lord says to pray without ceasing because the Lord knows better than you and me that prayer is very powerful.

The Lord says to pray without ceasing, and that truly always works for our good because we just don't know when the evil will come our way on any day.

Whenever I leave my house and get in my car, I pray to the Lord to help me to represent Him while I drive on the road.

I also pray to the Lord to help me to represent Him in the store where I shop for food.

One beautiful, sunny, warm day, I went to the store and when I went inside the Walmart store I heard a man talking close behind me.

I didn't look behind me to see if he was talking to someone on the phone, so I kept on walking while taking my time to get to the lane where I needed to go.

The young man who was close behind me had a grocery cart that he pushed up on the back of my left foot.

I stopped walking and quickly looked around at him with an angry look on my face as I said to him, "Look where you're going."

The young man said to me, "I am sorry," and then he touched my left arm and said you are a good man.

I was still a little angry at him and I said to him, "I thank the Lord," so he would know that it's the Lord who kept me in control of myself.

The young man recognized the Lord in me.

I truly believe that if I had not prayed to the Lord before I entered the Walmart store, then the situation would not have turned out good for me and him.

The Lord loves us both the same.

It's always good to pray without ceasing because prayer can surely keep you and me strong in the Lord when the devil tries his best to make trouble for us and make us angry at people who may not intentionally harm us.

Even if people intentionally do us wrong, prayer is still very powerful to keep us strong in the Lord and keep us calm so we make the devil angry that he didn't succeed in causing you and me to misrepresent the Lord in the presence of especially unbelievers.

Can't Take Away

People's criticism can't take away what the Lord has given to you.

People's silence can't take away what the Lord has given to you.

People's prejudice can't take away what the Lord has given to you.

People's hatred can't take away what the Lord has given to you.

People's tricks can't take away what the Lord has given to you.

People's lies can't take away what the Lord has given to you.

People's deceptions can't take away what the Lord has given to you.

People's jealousy can't take away what the Lord has given to you.

People's envy can't take away what the Lord has given to you.

People's greed can't take away what the Lord has given to you.

People's discouragement can't take away what the Lord has given to you.

People's rudeness can't take away what the Lord has given to you.

People's doubts can't take away what the Lord has given to you.

People's threats can't take away what the Lord has given to you.

People's disloyalty can't take away what the Lord has given to you.

People's carelessness can't take away what the Lord has given to you.

People's neglect can't take away what the Lord has given to you.

People's confusion can't take away what the Lord has given to you.

People's drama can't take away what the Lord has given to you.

People's pride can't take away what the Lord has given to you.

People's achievements can't take away what the Lord has given to you.

People's wealth can't take away what the Lord has given to you.

People's education can't take away what the Lord has given to you.

People's fame can't take away what the Lord has given to you.

People's pretense can't take away what the Lord has given to you.

People's false doctrines can't take away what the Lord has given to you.

People's selfishness can't take away what the Lord has given to you.

People's failures can't take away what the Lord has given to you.

People's motives can't take away what the Lord has given to you.

People's intentions can't take away what the Lord has given to you.

People's theories can't take away what the Lord has given to you.

People's plans can't take away what the Lord has given to you.

People's educated guesses can't take away what the Lord has given to you.

People's choices can't take away what the Lord has given to you.

If the Lord gives you talents, no one can take them away from you.

If the Lord gives you skills, no one can take them away from you.

If the Lord gives you genius, no one can take it away from you.

If the Lord gives you intelligence, no one can take it away from you.

If the Lord gives you common sense, no one can take it away from you.

If the Lord gives you spiritual gifts, no one can take them away from you.

You can surely take away what the Lord gives to you if you put anyone above the Lord.

You can surely take away what the Lord gives to you if you put anything above the Lord.

You and I will take away our own blessings from the Lord if we do our own will and live our lives in the foolishness of sin.

You can't blame anyone else for taking away what the Lord give to you, when you can choose to seek the Lord, who you can surely find in His holy Word.

You can only blame yourself for taking away what the Lord gives to you to use to glorify and magnify His holy name.

People's unconcerned ways can't take away what the Lord gives to you.

If the Lord is for you, who can be against you and take away what the Lord gives to you?

The Lord Jesus Christ will never give you and me anything that is bad that will cause our souls to be lost or anyone else's soul to be lost in hell.

What the Lord gives to you is for your good and for the good of others to be saved in Him.

Adam and Eve

Adam and Eve must have broken down and cried hard when they realized they had made a big mess of things by eating that forbidden fruit from the tree of good, knowledge and evil.

Adam and Eve must have cried real hard when Cain killed his brother Abel because God didn't accept his offerings.

Adam and Eve must have cried real hard when they saw the animals fighting and killing some of the other animals.

Adam and Eve must have cried real hard because they knew that many of their descendants would be murderers and disobedient to their parents.

Adam and Eve must have cried real hard when they realized that many of their descendants would be greedy for worldly gain.

Adam and Eve must have cried real hard when they realized that many of their descendants would be adulterers and fornicators.

Adam and Eve must have cried real hard when they realized that many of their descendants would be liars and covetous.

Adam and Eve must have cried real hard when they realized that many of their descendants would be lost in their sins.

Adam and Eve must have cried real hard when they realized that many of their descendants would be idol worshippers.

Adam and Eve must have cried real hard out loud together when they realized that they had disobeyed God, who told them to stay away from that tree of good, knowledge and evil that was in the midst of the Garden of Eden.

Adam and Eve must have cried real hard together when they realized that they had to leave the Garden of Eden for even touching that forbidden fruit.

God didn't leave Adam and Eve all alone, because God had promised them He would redeem them back to Him through His Son, Jesus

Christ, who would crush the serpent's head so it had no more power over all human beings who were saved in Him.

Adam and Eve must have cried real hard out loud together when they realized the evil they did would cause all of their children to suffer due to their disobedience against God.

Adam and Eve must have cried real hard out loud together more times than once because they knew they had caused all the world to suffer in darkness for thousands of years.

This must have tortured them, even in their dreams.

Adam and Eve must have cried real hard out loud together with so much joy and thanks unto God for allowing them to live for hundreds of years after their fall into sin that the second Adam didn't fall into.

Jesus Christ was without sin and gave up His life on the cross to save all sinful human beings from our sins.

Jesus was the second Adam.

Adam and Eve must have broken down and cried real hard to God and asked Him to forgive them for giving up their dominion over the world to the devil, who must have laughed at them real hard.

Adam and Eve must have cried out loud real hard together when they realized they had the rest of their lives to see that what God told them was right from the beginning of their lives that they had cut short by disobeying God in the Garden of Eden.

On the Stage of this World

Our walk with Jesus must be real on the stage of this world.

A stage is a place for the audience to watch very intently to see the performers giving them their best acting skills to captivate their fullest attention.

On the stage of this world, God loves to see realness in His children and wants them to be real about Him with no play-acting.

Our faith in Jesus must be real on the stage of this world.

Our love for Jesus must be real on the stage of this world.

Our love for even our enemies must be real on the stage of this world.

Even other worlds are watching you and me who call ourselves Christians.

Other worlds love to see real, true Christians on the stage of this world.

There are no rehearsals on the stage of this world.

God didn't give us free will choices to be rehearsed on the stage of this world.

Our free will choices are spontaneous to God on the stage of this world.

Our free will choices are so real to God all the time, but many people think of their free will choices like a prink on the stage of this world.

We Christians are under the limelight for the people of the world to see if we are real about Jesus Christ on the stage of this world.

The limelight of God's Commandments can surely illuminate the truth about the way we should live our lives on the stage of this world.

There are many stages where people can rehearse and perform with extraordinary skills for people to be captivated and spellbound by their performances.

There is only one stage of this world where everybody will be watched by the angels, other worlds and, most of all, be watched by God.

This will be no stage show because God is always real and wants real, true Christians to be like His Son, Jesus Christ.

Jesus was under the limelight on the stage of this world, and no one else will ever get an audience like Jesus because all the holy angels, all the fallen angels, all the other worlds and God Himself watched Jesus so intensely as He was beaten and bruised and was nailed to the cross so real and died and rose again so real to redeem all mankind and womankind back to God.

You Can't be Sure About

You can't be sure about your wealth.

You can't be sure about your husband.

You can't be sure about your wife.

You can't be sure about your children.

You can't be sure about your house.

You can't be sure about your car.

You can't be sure about your truck.

You can't be sure about your airplane.

You can't be sure about your skills.

You can't be sure about your talents.

You can't be sure about your achievements.

You can't be sure about your education.

You can't be sure about your life.

You can't be sure about your dreams.

You can't be sure about your health.

You can't be sure about yourself.

You can't be sure about this world.

You can't be sure about your feelings.

You can't be sure about your mind.

You can't be sure about your heart.

You can't be sure about anything.

You can't be sure about anyone in this world.

You can only be sure about God the Father, the Son and the Holy Spirit.

You can only be sure about God's saving grace.

You can only be sure about the Lord and Savior Jesus Christ, who all of the angels in heaven are sure about.

You can be sure about God's holy Word.

You can be sure about God's mercy.

You can be sure about God's goodness that leads to repentance.

You can be sure about God's love.

You can be sure about God's forgiveness.

You can be sure about God's protection.

You can't be sure about your own words.

You can't be sure about what you see.

You can't be sure about what you hear.

You can't be sure about what you eat.

You can't be sure about what you drink.

You can't be sure about what you do.

You can only be sure about Jesus Christ, who can do anything but fail you and me.

You can't be sure about your friends.

You can't be sure about your family.

You can't be sure about your boyfriend.

You can't be sure about your girlfriend.

You can't be sure about your pets.

You can't be sure about your business.

You can't be sure about your pastor.

You can't be sure about your church family.

You can only be sure about Jesus Christ, who gave up His life on the cross and rose from the grave to save you and me from our sins if we confess and repent and love Jesus and keep His Commandments that we can be sure about every day.

You can't be sure about your computer.

You can't be sure about your iPhone.

You can't be sure about technology.

You can't be sure about science.

You can't be sure about evolution.

You can't be sure about your parents.

You can't be sure about your brothers and sisters.

You can only be sure about Jesus Christ, who loves you and me so much more than our blood kin.

You can only be sure about Jesus Christ, who created the heavens and earth with His perfect and infinite wisdom that is forevermore beyond this world's technology and science that is like a dried-up plum to Jesus.

You can't be sure about the past, present and future, but you can be sure about Jesus Christ coming back again to take you and me to heaven if we are saved in Him.

No Better Than

You are no better than me, and I am no better than you.

You need to eat food just like me, and I need to eat food just like you.

You need to drink water just like me, and I need to drink water just like you.

You need to take a shower just like me, and I need to take a shower just like you.

You are no better than me, and I am no better than you.

You need to brush your teeth just like me, and I need to brush my teeth just like you.

You need to work just like me, and I need to work just like you.

You need a roof over your head just like me, and I need a roof over my head just like you.

You can get sick just like me, and I can get sick just like you.

You need encouragement just like me, and I need encouragement just like you.

You need a good friend just like me, and I need a good friend just like you.

You need to read the Bible just like me, and I need to read the Bible just like you.

You need to love Jesus and keep His Commandments like me, and I need to love Jesus and keep His commandments like you.

You are no better than me, and I am no better than you.

You need to put on some clothes like me, and I need to put on some clothes like you.

You need to lay down to sleep like me, and I need to lay down to sleep like you.

You need to take good care of yourself like me, and I need to take your care of myself like you.

You need to put on some shoes like me, and I need to put on some shoes like you.

When Jesus comes back again, I will go to heaven with Him like you, and you will go to heaven with Him like me if we are saved in Jesus.

I am no better than you, and you are no better than me in the all-seeing eyes of our Lord God who created you and me in His image.

I can fall down like you, and you can fall down like me.

I can feel pain like you, and you can feel pain like me.

I can have dreams in my sleep like you, and you can have dreams in your sleep like me.

I can take a chance like you, and you can take a chance like me.

I can have good and bad thoughts like you, and you can have a good and bad thoughts like me.

I have a free will to choose like you, and you have a free will to choose like me.

I have a destiny like you, and you have a destiny like me.

Even though our destinies may be different, it's only for God to know whether my destiny is heaven and your destiny is hell or if my destiny is hell and your destiny is heaven.

I am no better than you, and you are no better than me in the eyes of Jesus, who shows no respect of persons to save you and me from being lost in our sins.

The "I" Word

The "I" word is not always about being proud.

The "I" word can also be a humble word to say.

You can say, "I love my wife," and that is not being proud.

You can say, "I love my husband," and that is not being proud.

You can say, "I love my children," and that is not being proud.

You can say, "I love my friends," and that is not being proud.

You can say, "I love my pets," and that is not being proud.

You can say, "I love everybody," and that is not being proud.

You can say, "I love the Lord," and that is not being proud.

You can say, "I will do the Lord's will," and that is not being proud.

You can say, "I love going to church," and that is not being proud.

The "I" word is not always about being proud.

You can say, "I love my job," and that is not being proud.

The "I" word can also be a humble word to say.

You can say, "I will confess and repent of my sins," and that is not being proud.

You can say, "I will hold onto the Lord," and that is not being proud.

You can say, "I love to pray," and that is not being proud.

You can say, "I love to give God all the glory and praise," and that is not being proud.

The "I" word can be a humble word to say.

The "I" word is not always about being proud.

You can say, "I will humble myself into the Lord," and that is not being proud.

Many people will say the "I" word to make themselves look good.

Many people will say the "I" word to draw attention to themselves.

Lucifer said "I will ascend above the stars in heaven," and that was a proud way to use the "I" word.

The "I" word can be used for good and it can be used for evil.

The Truth will Not Always Make Us Feel Good

The truth will not always make us feel good, especially if someone is stepping on our toes with the truth.

The truth will not always make us feel good, but the truth will set us free from even lying to ourselves.

The truth will not always make us feel good, but the truth is the best words to hear day after day.

The truth will not always make us feel good, but the truth can help us to change for the better.

The truth will not always make us feel good, but the truth is like taking good medicine to help us to get well.

The truth will not always make us feel good, but the truth is joy to anyone who loves the truth.

The truth will not always make us feel good, but the truth will set us free from the devil's lies.

The truth will not always make us feel good, but the truth will stand up strong against any lie.

The truth will not always make us feel good, but the truth won't change on anyone.

The truth will not always make us feel good, but the truth is always good to us to hold onto.

The truth will not always make us feel good, but the truth of God's holy word is sharper than a two-edged sword.

The truth will not always make us feel good, but the truth of God's holy word can surely prolong our lives.

The truth will not always make us feel good, but the truth of God's holy word will never change.

The truth will not always make us feel good, but the truth of God's holy word can surely heal our sin-sick souls.

The truth will not always make us feel good, but the truth of God's holy word is everlasting truth for us to always believe.

The truth will not always make us feel good, but the truth of God's word points us to Jesus Christ, who is the way the truth and the life for all to believe in and be saved from our sins that originated from the devil's lies.

For Thousands of Years

For thousands of years the devil has been trying to destroy the marriage between a man and a woman.

For thousands of years the devil has been trying to destroy heterosexual relationships.

For thousands of years the devil has been trying to destroy healthy born babies.

For thousands of years the devil has been trying to destroy good friendships.

For thousands of years the devil has been trying to destroy love.

For thousands of years the devil has been trying to destroy peace.

For thousands of years the devil has been trying to destroy joy.

For thousands of years the devil has been trying to destroy hope.

For thousands of years the devil has been trying to destroy faith.

For thousands of years the devil has been trying to destroy grace.

For thousands of years the devil has been trying to destroy temperance.

For thousands of years the devil has been trying to destroy strength.

For thousands of years the devil has been trying to destroy justice.

For thousands of years the devil has been trying to destroy equality.

For thousands of years the devil has been trying to destroy freedom.

For thousands of years the devil has been trying to destroy order.

For thousands of years the devil has been trying to destroy conviction.

For thousands of years the devil has been trying to destroy conversion.

For thousands of years the devil has been trying to destroy truth.

For thousands of years the devil has been trying to destroy the Ten Commandments.

For thousands of years the devil has been trying to destroy the true church.

For thousands of years the devil has been trying to destroy the holy word of God.

For thousands of years the devil has been trying to destroy life.

For thousands of years the devil has failed all of his attempts to destroy this world that still exists because of Jesus Christ, who will one day destroy the devil and his fallen angels and human agents in fire and brimstone.

For thousands of years the devil has been trying to destroy the family.

For thousands of years the devil has been trying to destroy good health.

For thousands of years the devil has been trying to destroy wisdom.

For thousands of years the devil has been trying to destroy beauty.

For thousands of years the devil has been trying to destroy common sense.

For thousands of years the devil has been trying to destroy bravery.

For thousands of years the devil has been trying to destroy speaking good words.

For thousands of years the devil has been trying to destroy doing good deeds.

For thousands of years the devil has been trying to destroy humility.

For thousands of years the Lord Jesus Christ has been trying to save as many souls as He can, because Jesus knows that everyone will not believe in Him to be saved from the devil who is a thief, a murder, and a liar just like he has been for thousands of years here on earth.

This Day

O Lord, I think You for blessing me to live to see this day that thousands of years ago can't compare to.

O Lord, I think You for blessing me to live to see this day that hundreds of years ago can't compare to.

O Lord, I think You for blessing me to live to see this day that decades ago can't compare to.

O Lord, I think You for blessing me to live to see this day that a year ago can't compare to.

O Lord, I think You for blessing me to live to see this day that a month ago can't compare to.

O Lord, I think You for blessing me to live to see this day that a week ago can't compare to.

O Lord, I think You for blessing me to live to see this day that yesterday can't compare to.

This day may be a thousand years away from the end of this world.

This day may be a hundred years away from the end of this world.

This day may be a decade away from the end of this world.

This day may be a year away from the close of God's probation on this world.

This day may be a month away from the close of God's probation on this world.

This day may be a week away from the close of God's probation on this world.

This day may be one day away from the close of God's probation on this world.

O Lord, I think you for blessing me to live to see this day that my past sinful life can't compare to.

O Lord, I think you for blessing me to live to see this day that my yesterdays can't compare to.

O Lord, I think you for blessing me to live to see this day that my past ignorance can't compare to this day that I don't deserve to know the truth of Your holy word that has set me free from the devil's lies.

This day is like eternity to me, whose alive above the grave where there is no consciousness of life to know anything.

O Lord, I thank You for blessing me to be alive this day that my destiny is sealed in the choices that I make today.

It only takes this day for me to choose life or death.

It only takes this day for me to choose Jesus or the devil.

O Lord, I thank You for blessing me to be alive this day that I can die, because I know that a thousand years are like just one day to You, O Lord.

You will wake me up again in the first resurrection or in the second resurrection which can be like only tomorrow to you, O Lord.

O Lord, I think you for blessing me to be alive this day that I can choose to love You and keep Your Commandments that will destine me to enter into heaven when You come back again, which will be a day that only God knows when this day is unpredictable to me and not to God.

O Lord, I thank you for blessing me to live to see this day, and only You will know how this day will be for me who can give You, O Lord, my all this day.

O Lord, I thank You for blessing me to live to see this day that is a miracle from You, O Lord, for me to see.

O Lord, I thank You for blessing me to live to see this day that all the living surround me and know that life is from You, who gives it to me to enjoy living my life unto You, my Lord, no matter what this day will bring to me.

O Lord, I thank You for blessing me to live to see this day that no one can take away from me without Your approval that is guaranteed to be for my good, even unto my death.

O Lord, I thank You for blessing me to live to see this day that is more real than all of my yesterdays that are gone like they never happened, because this day is what really matters to my soul's salvation for me to be saved in You, O Lord.

O Lord, I thank You for blessing me to live to see this day that is so far away from thousands of years ago, even though this day surely has the same sunshine as it did thousands of years ago.

O Lord, I thank You for blessing me to live to see this day that has the same sky like thousands of years ago.

O Lord, I thank You for blessing me to live to see this day that has the same invisible air like thousands of years ago.

O Lord, I thank You for blessing me to live to see this day that is presence of life like thousands of years ago.

O Lord, I thank You for blessing me to live to see this day that lets me know that You, O Lord, are not finished with me yet and I won't be going to the land of the dead this day.

This day is like eternity to me for being alive to choose to live for You, my Lord and Savior Jesus Christ, who this day I love and obey even through deep distresses that can't overrule Your supreme authority over this day, O Lord.

God Named the Days

God named the days the first day, the second day, the third day, the fourth day, the fifth day, the sixth day and the seventh day.

Man named the first day Sunday, the second day Monday, the third day Tuesday, the fourth day Wednesday, the fifth day Thursday, the sixth day Friday and the seventh day Saturday on the calendar.

The seventh day in the bible is Saturday on the manmade calendar.

God rested from all of His creation on the seventh day of the week that God made holy and apart from the other six days of the week.

God commands us all to keep the seventh day holy and says not to work.

The seventh day of the week is the holy Sabbath day of rest.

The holy Sabbath day of rest is not only a physical rest but also a spiritual rest for us to rest our minds in the Lord and give Him worship and all the glory and praise in the household of faith.

God gave the original names of the days to Moses, who God had inspired to write the book of Genesis giving us all the correct names of the days.

The first day, the second day, the third day, the fourth day, the fifth day, the sixth day and the seventh day are named by God from the beginning of time here on earth.

The God-named days that will never change in His holy word, even though rebellious human beings have changed the holy Sabbath day of rest from Saturday to Sunday.

God had nothing to do with this change.

Only rebellious human beings will try to make it look like God approves of their made-up move of the holy Sabbath day of rest to Sunday.

I am Only Human

Many people love to say, "I am only human," so they can do what they want to do.

Many people love to say, "I am only human," so they have an excuse to not want to change for the better.

Many people love to say, "I am only human," as if the Lord can't help them to overcome their human problems.

Jesus left all of heaven to become a human being so He could relate to us human beings.

Jesus gave up all of heaven to become a human being without sin to save us human beings from our sins.

You and I can't be more human than Jesus was when He lived here on earth among sinful human beings.

Jesus knows all about being human, and He knows more than you and I will ever know because He was a human being who was tempted by all of the devil's temptations.

You and I will never be tempted by all of the devil's temptations because Jesus made a way for us to escape from the devil's worst temptations that our human lives wouldn't be able to handle.

Many people love to say, "I am only human," as if Jesus was never a human being sent to ease their minds from worrying about things that Jesus can work out and remove like they never existed.

Saying, "I am only human," is disrespecting Jesus, who we have no excuse to doubt because of all the things He can do for us in our distress.

Jesus was human and there is nothing that Jesus didn't go through to give us the strength to overcome our human deficiencies.

You and I can easily say, "I am only human," as if the Lord doesn't know that we have human weaknesses.

We cannot use "I am only human" as an excuse to not put all of our trust in the Lord to be there for us who can't trust our human ways to comfort us.

Jesus can always comfort us in our human misfortunes.

The Only Good Thing About War

The only good thing about war is that the good nation wins the war.

There is nothing good about especially good soldiers getting killed.

There is nothing good about especially good soldiers getting wounded.

The only good thing about war is that the good nation wins the war.

There is nothing good about civilian people getting badly wounded in a war.

There is nothing good about civilian people killed in a war.

The only good thing about war is that the good nation wins the war.

When a good nation of people wins a war, God is surely on their side every step of the way.

There is nothing good about shedding innocent blood in a war, no matter if the people live in a good nation or a bad nation.

If the good nation wins the war, all the people in the good nation can be joyful about their victory.

The very first war was up in heaven where the good angels outnumbered the evil angels and won the war in heaven.

Michael the archangel who was Jesus Christ was in full command of the good angels, and Jesus led the charge to a great victory over Lucifer and his evil angels.

There will be a great victory for you and me and all the holy saints one day when Jesus rains down fire and brimstone on the devil and all the evil angels and all of the devil's human agents.

They will surround the new Jerusalem holy city and will fail in their evil mission because of Jesus Christ, who will destroy them all in hell's fire and brimstone.

If the good nation wins the war, even the civilian people in a bad nation can reap the good benefits because God is good to bless the good nation to show mercy on the civilian people in a bad nation and let them live and know that God is good to them.

Jesus Made a Hostage Deal for You and Me

Jesus made a hostage deal to save you and me from being lost in our sins that Jesus became on the cross to be the hostage deal with sin.

Jesus made a hostage deal with the devil when He was spit on and beaten and whipped until He bled to take on our infirmities.

Jesus made a hostage deal with eternal death when He shed His blood on the cross and died on the cross in our place as He rose from the grave to set us free from eternal death for being saved in Him.

Jesus made a hostage deal with this sinful world for you and me to not be a captive to sin that's been holding all human beings hostages of sin since the fall of Adam and Eve.

No one will ever make a better hostage deal than Jesus Christ, who made the greatest hostage deal for you and me when He got the victory over death and the grave to give you and me eternal life when he comes back again.

God made a hostage deal with death and the grave when His Son, Jesus Christ, died for our sins and lay down in the grave where He was held captive.

The hostage deal that God made with death and the grave was that death and the grave wanted God to turn His back on His Son, which God did for only two days.

The devil just didn't know that God would raise Jesus from the grave to set every human hostage free from being lost in sin.

The devil and death and the grave had believed that they made an eternal hostage deal with God, but it's not in God's nature to allow anything that's not like Him to exist forever and ever.

Jesus made a hostage deal for you and me and all the world to be saved in Him who truly knows that the devil's hostage deals are never fair to not make anyone happy.

Nobody Can
Keep Up with the Lord

Nobody can keep up with the Lord and know how far the Lord will allow anyone to go in life.

Nobody can keep up with the Lord to see what the Lord sees coming into anyone's life.

Nobody can keep up with the Lord who doesn't overlook anyone to save from being lost in sin.

Nobody can keep up with the Lord to know what will happen, even in the next second that the Lord can stop it from happening and spare anyone's life from death.

Nobody can keep up with the Lord who understands every word that anyone says because the Lord created every language in this world.

Nobody can keep up with the Lord who knows everybody's motives and intentions that can't fool the Lord.

Nobody can keep up with the Lord who the Pharisees couldn't outsmart or trick because the Lord Jesus Christ was always ahead of them and knew their hearts.

Nobody can keep up with the Lord and get ahead of the Lord's will with one's own will that's like a bubble that bursts in the thin air to the Lord.

Nobody can keep up with the Lord who is always ahead of anyone to stop someone's evil deeds from spreading like wildfire.

Nobody can keep up with the Lord who is present beyond the countless stars in every galaxy that nobody can go to because our lives are so short to an eternal Lord God who is the ancient of days to never age or grow old before the countless stars that only the Lord knows the true age of in every universe.

Nobody can keep up with the Lord who knows everybody who will go to heaven with Him when He comes back again and will not be surprised by anyone who will be lost out of heaven.

You and I will be surprised to enter into heaven and be surprised to see who we believe to be lost.

You and I will also be surprised to not see who we believe will enter into heaven.

Nobody can keep up with the Lord Jesus Christ who the devil couldn't keep up with to keep Jesus in the grave, because that was impossible for the devil to do.

God's Ambassadors

We Christians are God's ambassadors on earth where we are supposed to spread the gospel of Jesus Christ and win souls to Him.

We Christians are God's ambassadors on earth where we are supposed to love Jesus and keep His Commandments in the presence of the people of the world.

We Christians are God's ambassadors on earth where we are supposed to live right by example.

The sun is God's ambassador in the universe.

The moon is God's ambassador in the universe.

The stars are God's ambassadors in the universe.

The galaxies are God's ambassadors in the universe.

The black holes are God's ambassadors in the universe.

The planets are God's ambassadors in the universe.

The solar system is God's ambassador in the universe.

The meteors are God's ambassadors in the universe.

The universe is God's ambassador in the universe.

Other worlds are God's ambassadors.

They all represent God's creation beyond this world.

The holy angels are God's ambassadors in heaven above the universe.

Ambassadors are the highest-ranking representatives of their country.

Ambassadors are the greatest representatives of their country's policies.

God's ambassadors represent God's Son, Jesus Christ, in this world that is foreign to you and me for being a Christian.

God's ambassadors in heaven and the universe and in other worlds and on earth are God's joyous representatives, giving God's Son, Jesus Christ, all the glory and praise and worship because He is worthy to sit on the right-hand side of God's holy throne forever and ever.

The sky is God's ambassador to represent this world.

Nature is God's ambassador to represent this world.

The elements in the earth are God's ambassadors to represent this world.

Ambassadors are the highest representatives for any nation.

We Christians are ambassadors of God.

We Christians are the highest representatives of God here on earth.

Jesus Christ, our Lord and Savior, is the ambassador of God in heaven where Jesus once came from to represent God's love here on earth as he was bruised for our iniquities and wounded for our transgressions.

Jesus is God's ambassador who had shed His blood and died on the cross to become sin in our place.

Jesus is God's ambassador who rose from the grave with the victory over death and the grave.

There is no greater ambassador than Jesus Christ, who represents God's love to all the world, to all the other worlds, to all the universes and to all existence seen and unseen.

Jesus Christ is God's ambassador in heaven where all the angels bow down before Him and give Him all the glory and praise for creating them and all things visible and invisible.

For what have human beings created that Jesus can't destroy when He will create a new heaven and new earth beyond this world that will pass away one day along with everything in it.

Jesus is God's ambassador to represent God's supreme power and rulership over all creatures that Jesus created.

Each of us is an ambassador of our own free will choices that we represent every day in our words and actions before one another and Jesus.

Only Jesus always knows the motives and intentions of our hearts, because Jesus is the ambassador of our hearts and represents you and me in the presence of God.

You Chose Me to Follow You

In my messed up mind, You chose me to follow You, O Lord.

In my broken spirit, You chose me to follow You, O Lord.

In my selfish heart, You chose me to follow You, O Lord.

In my wandering ways, You chose me to follow You, O Lord.

In my ups and downs in life, You chose me to follow You, O Lord.

In my bad motives, You chose me to follow You, O Lord.

In my bad intentions, You chose me to follow You, O Lord.

In my fears, You chose me to follow You, O Lord.

In my failures, You chose me to follow You, O Lord.

In my discouragements, You chose me to follow You, O Lord.

In my disappointments, You chose me to follow You, O Lord.

In my carelessness, You chose me to follow You, O Lord.

In my guilt, You chose me to follow You, O Lord.

In my sorrow, You chose me to follow You, O Lord.

In my loneliness, You chose me to follow You, O Lord.

In my cheerfulness, You chose me to follow You, O Lord.

In my achievements, You chose me to follow You, O Lord.

In my doubts, You chose me to follow You, O Lord.

In my hardships, You chose me to follow You, O Lord.

In my distress, You chose me to follow You, O Lord.

In my pride, You chose me to follow You, O Lord.

In my free will choices, You chose me to follow You, O Lord.

In my ignorance of You, You chose me to follow You, O Lord.

You chose me, O Lord, so long before I was born.

You chose me, O Lord, when I was living in my sins.

You chose me, O Lord, before I chose to believe in You.

You chose me, O Lord, when I gave up on living.

You chose me, O Lord, to follow You even if I don't choose to, which will surely be my eternal doom.

You chose me, O Lord, as if I was the only sinner living in a world with perfect people.

In my imperfections, You chose me to follow You, O Lord.

In my bad habits, You chose me to follow You, O Lord.

In my mistakes, You chose me to follow You, O Lord.

In my downfalls, You chose me to follow You, O Lord.

In my unbelief, You chose me to follow You, O Lord.

In my disobedience, You chose me to follow you, O Lord.

In my denial, You chose me to follow You, O Lord.

Peter denied You three times, but You chose Peter to follow You, O Lord.

In my lifetime, You chose me to follow You, O Lord.

In my past, present and future, You chose me to follow You, my Lord and Savior Jesus Christ.

You choosing me to follow You, O Lord, was before You created this world with my name that You want to write down in Your book of life when I must choose to follow You, O Lord, for You to not blot out my name in Your book of life.

O, my Lord and Savior Jesus Christ, You chose everybody to follow You no matter what condition they are in.

O, my Lord, You chose everybody to follow You, even though not all of them will chose to follow You who will never lead anyone away from eternal life.

If you and I follow the devil, he will lead us to eternal death.

In my wondering of not knowing what this day has in store for me, You chose me to follow You, my Lord and Savior Jesus Christ, as if this is my last day to live.

I can only pray and hope that You, O Lord, will allow me to live many more years doing Your holy will.

O Lord, I don't want to follow behind this world anymore.

This world has led me into brokenness.

O Lord, I don't want to follow behind this world anymore.

This world has led me into hopelessness.

O Lord, I don't want to follow behind this world anymore.

This world has led me into heartaches.

O Lord, I don't want to follow behind this world anymore.

This world has led me into grief.

O Lord, I don't want to follow behind this world anymore.

This world has led me into deceptions.

O Lord, I don't want to follow behind this world anymore.

This world has led me into living in the darkness of my sins.

In my wayward life, You chose me, O Lord, to follow You, when I just didn't know that I was gambling my soul with the devil who knew that You chose me to follow You, O Lord.

O Lord, You chose me to follow You who gave me a choice to follow You.

The devil can't stack the card deck with his tricks to keep me from choosing to follow You, O Lord, who gives me the winning hand of the free will choice for me to choose to follow You who chose me to follow You before You created the heavens and earth.

O Lord, I Can Never

O Lord, I can never pray to You enough.

O Lord, I can never speak about to You enough.

O Lord, I can never give enough of testimonies about You.

O Lord, I can never be enough of a witness of You.

O Lord, I can never trust You enough.

O Lord, I can never uplift Your holy name enough.

O Lord, I can never love You enough.

O Lord, I can never obey You enough.

O Lord, I can never call on Your holy name enough.

O Lord, I can never believe in You enough.

O Lord, I can never do enough of work for You.

O Lord, I can never live for You enough.

O Lord, I can never praise You enough.

O Lord, I can never worship You enough.

O Lord, I can never glorify You enough.

O Lord, I can never humble myself unto You enough.

O Lord, I can never study Your holy word enough.

O Lord, I can never follow You enough.

O Lord, I can never know You enough.

O Lord, I can never have enough of a relationship with You.

O Lord, I can never hear enough about You.

O Lord, I can never confess and repent of my sins enough unto You.

O Lord, I can never keep Your Commandments enough.

O Lord, I can never need enough of Your blessings.

O Lord, I can never need enough of Your mercy.

O Lord, I can never need enough of Your grace.

O Lord, I can never need enough of Your protection.

O Lord, I can never need enough of Your wisdom.

O Lord, I can never need enough of Your love.

O Lord, I can never need enough of Your forgiveness.

O Lord, I can never need enough of Your holiness.

O Lord, I can never need enough of Your righteousness.

O Lord, I can never need enough of You supplying all of my needs.

O Lord, I can never give You enough of my heart.

O Lord, I can never give You enough of my soul.

O Lord, I can never give You enough of my life.

O Lord, I can never give You enough of my best.

O Lord, I can never give You enough of my all, because I was born in sin to fall short of Your glory that is enough for me to truly know that I can never need enough of Your Holy Spirit.

O Lord, I can never need enough of Your salvation for as long as I live because I must be saved in You, O Lord, to go with You to heaven when You come back again.

O, my Lord and Savior Jesus Christ, I will never get enough of heaven because of You being there filling up heaven with God's everlasting love that I will never get enough of throughout my eternal life.

O Lord, I was never too lost in my sins enough for You to not find me and bring me back to You, O Lord, who is forevermore than enough for me to not deserve to be saved in You.

O Lord, I never exist enough in this world for You, O Lord, to not know my destiny that is enough for You to seal.

I can never make You my choice enough, O Lord, in this rebellious world that is against You.

O Lord, You can never get enough of saving me from my sins and cleansing me of my sins to represent my case before God in heaven.

I can never be enough like You, O Lord, on my own righteousness being like filthy rags to You, O Lord, every day.

Who Am I to Question You, O Lord?

Who am I to question You, O Lord, about why You allow bad things to happen in this world?

Who am I to question You, O Lord, about why You allow good people to suffer hardships?

Who am I to question You, O Lord, about why You allow many young people to die?

Who am I to question You, O Lord, about why You allow my enemies to degrade me?

Who am I to question You, O Lord, about why You allow the rich to get richer and the poor to get poorer?

Who am I to question You, O Lord, about why You allow the wheat and tares in the church to grow together?

Who am I to question You, O Lord, about why You haven't come back yet?

Who am I to question You, O Lord, about why I have to put up with some selfish and proud church folks?

Who am I to question You, O Lord, about why You allowed me to make it this far in life?

Who am I to question You, O Lord, about why You even put up with me?

Who am I to question You, O Lord, about why You allow some criminals to get away with their crimes?

Who am I to question You, O Lord, about why You allow many people to be prejudiced against another race of people?

Who am I to question You, O Lord, about why You allow many innocent children, women and men to get killed in war?

Who am I to question You, O Lord, about why You allow many people to break the laws of the land?

Who am I to question You, O Lord, about why You allowed sinful men to crucify You on the cross?

Who am I to question You, O Lord, about what You said to Job: "Where were you when I laid down the foundations of the earth?"

Job got his answer from the Lord God, whose answer was so profound to Job that he never questioned God again.

God questioned Job, but Job couldn't give God a good answer to His question.

This goes to show that God always knows what to do for our soul's salvation in Him through his Son, Jesus Christ, who existed before anything in heaven and on earth.

Who am I to question You, O Lord, who sees all things, knows all things and can do all things when I can be questioned and have no answer to give?

Everything Will Not Be Perfect All the Time

No matter how many times we rehearse our script for a play, we can make a mistake and say something or do something that's not in the script.

Everything will not be perfect all the time in our lives.

No matter how good your memory is, you can still forget something because everything will not be perfect all the time.

It's so easy to see someone else's imperfections, but we all have some imperfections because we were born in sin to have a sinful nature that is far from perfection.

We can strongly believe that we have ourselves so well put together that we're perfect, until we get caught off guard and say or do something wrong and we don't even understand why we said or did something wrong.

Everything will not be perfect in our lives all the time because we are sinners and have flaws and imperfections in our lives every day.

No matter how well we rehearse our script for a part in a play, we can still leave out a word or two and the audience might not even pick up on it or see our imperfection.

Those who have rehearsed with you and me will pretty much know what we said wrong or what we did wrong before the audience.

There are even times that some people in the audience will see what we did wrong, even though they were not in on our rehearsals for our part in the play.

We can want to say everything perfectly and we can want to do everything perfectly, but that will not happen in this imperfect world where we are all imperfect people needing a perfect Lord and Savior who is Jesus Christ to be our part in the play of life.

If we mess up on our part we may feel so bad about that, but Jesus can surely remove this bad feeling from us If we pray to Him and ask Him to give us the strength to move beyond our errors that the devil loves to use against us to make us feel bad.

Everything will not be perfect all the time for you and me, but we can surely trust Jesus to help us to not look back on the things that we said wrong or did wrong, whether we rehearsed them or not.

If anyone holds our wrongs against us who are saved in Jesus Christ, they hold it against Jesus as well.

Jesus is perfect to have no sins and He can cleanse anyone from their sins.

Any perfectionist doesn't see the need to admit that they can make a mistake, and they will be in denial.

They only fool themselves into thinking they are perfect, when they are not perfect.

Everything will be perfect all the time for our Lord and Savior Jesus Christ who is not hard on us for making a mistake, even though we can be hard on ourselves for making a mistake.

We can rehearse our script for a play and believe that we have it all figured out to move the audience, but we can be at risk of making a mistake because of being born in sin and having some imperfections, even in our genetic makeup.

The Eternal Age of God

It is like we don't exist at all compared to the eternal age of God.

It is like we were never born compared to the eternal age of God.

It is like this world doesn't exist compared to the eternal age of God.

It is like a thousand years never passed by compared to the eternal age of God.

It is like a billion years never passed by compared to the eternal age of God.

It is like a trillion years never passed by compared to the eternal age of God.

It is like all the light years in the galaxies don't exist compared to the eternal age of God.

It is like nothing exists at all compared to the eternal age of God.

The eternal age of God is forever younger than any new born baby.

A new born baby can be one day old, but the age of God has no number of days, weeks, months or years.

We can number our days and watch ourselves age and get old, but no one can number God's days because God is all-eternal and never ages or gets old on our calendar days, weeks, months and years.

The eternal age of God is not down on our level of believing that all the light years in the outer space are eternal to us.

All the light years in the outer space are like only a moment to God.

We know that only a moment to God can be like a trillion years gone by.

It is like our time on earth is one second compared to the eternal age of God that has no man-made days, weeks, months and years.

God's is eternal and He is the ancient of days.

All the light years in the outer space can't compare to God's eternal existence.

The eternal age of God can show profound geniuses and brilliant minds in the technology and astronomy fields that there is a higher intelligence that was around before the beginning of time on earth and before the beginning of the universe.

To be Exactly Like You

Would you love for someone to smack their lips at the same time that you smack your lips?

Would you love for someone to talk at the same time that you talk?

Would you love for someone to joke at the same time that you joke?

Would you love for someone to bite their nails at the same time that you bite your nails?

Would you love for someone to be exactly like you?

Would you love for someone to make a mistake at the same time that you make a mistake?

Would you love for someone to dig up their nose at the same time that you dig up your nose?

Would you love for someone to be disappointed at the same time that you are disappointed?

Would you love for someone to fall down at the same time that you fall down?

Would you love for someone to get angry at the same time that you get angry?

Would you love for someone to get choked at the same time that you get choked?

Would you love for someone to spit at the same time that you spit?

Would you love for someone to scratch their head at the same time that you scratch your head?

Would you love for someone to be afraid at the same time that you are afraid?

Would you love for someone to be exactly like you?

Would you love for someone to use the toilet at the same time that you use the toilet?

Would you love for someone's breath to smell exactly the same time as your breath?

Would you love for someone to feel some pain at the same time that you feel pain?

Would you love for someone to think all the same thoughts that you think?

Would you love for someone to say all the same words that you say?

Would you love for someone to feel all the same emotions that you feel?

Would you love for someone to do all the same things that you do?

Would you love for someone to be exactly like you?

No two people are exactly alike because God created everyone to be different with wonderful talents and gifts in the church.

If God had created everybody exactly alike, this world would be so void of being different and no one would make different choices.

Would you love for someone to be exactly like you who is not perfect and has sins to confess and repent unto the Lord Jesus Christ?

There is a Cost to Call Things Our Own

There is a cost to call things our own that belongs to the Lord who owns everything in heaven and here on earth.

If we want to call things our own that belong to the Lord, then we have to pay the Lord to own them.

So, how can we afford to pay the Lord who owns you and me and all things throughout the universe and other worlds that the Lord owns?

There is a cost to call something our own, because the Lord owns the air we breathe in and out of our nostrils every day.

If we want to call things our own, then we must be prepared to pay the Lord for even the ground we walk on and act like we own the ground the Lord owns every day and every night.

We want to call things our own and as soon as we have problems with what we call our own, we get frustrated and maybe want to disown those things, but the Lord can always handle them with no problem, day after day.

There is a cost to call things our own that we cannot take with us to the grave, and the grave doesn't have enough room for those things to fit into.

There's a cost to call things our own and that cost is too high for you and me to pay the Lord who owns all existence, seen and unseen.

The Lord owned all things before you and I were born.

We know nothing and can't do anything, but the Lord foreknew that you and I would want to call things our own even though they belong to the Lord who lives forever and ever and will never lose anything He owns.

Your Children Will Make Some Mistakes

Your children will make some mistakes in their lives no matter how good they are.

Your children will make some mistakes in their lives no matter how smart they are.

You can only pray that they won't make a mistake unto their death.

You can do all you can to raise your children right, but that won't be enough to keep them from making some mistakes in their lives.

No one has a perfect child who will do everything right all the time.

When Jesus was a little child, He had no sins and did everything right all the time because Jesus was the only sinless child who ever lived in this world.

You can love your children and teach them good words to say and good deeds to do, but they will still make some mistakes in their lives because they are not perfect and have sins to say something wrong and do something wrong when you may least expect it.

It is always good to raise your children doing the Lord's will, because that will surely help your children to make a lot of good choices in their lives.

Raising your children in the Lord won't exempt them from making some mistakes in their lives, but they will know what it means to get their lives back on track with the Lord since they know what is right because they were taught in the home and in the church.

There are big grown-up children and there are little children who will make some mistakes in their lives that Jesus can change for the better, no matter if their parents are not Christians.

When it comes to the Lord, we are all like little children needing the Lord's guidance and corrections through His holy word that is even for little children to know and live by every day.

Many grown-up children and many little children have made a mistake unto their death and many parents will blame God for that when it's the devil who loves to take anyone's life, no matter what age they are.

No Matter What Country You Are From

If you are white; you are white, no matter what country you are from.

If you are brown; you are brown, no matter what country you are from.

If you are black; you are black, no matter what country you are from.

There is no color barrier to Jesus, who gave up His life on the cross to save all white, brown and black sinners from being lost in their sins.

If you are white, Jesus loves you.

If you are brown, Jesus loves you.

If you are black, Jesus loves you.

If you are white, Jesus will judge you.

If you are brown, Jesus will judge you.

If you are black, Jesus will judge you.

No matter what country you are from, if you are white you must answer to Jesus.

No matter what country you are from, if you are brown you must answer to Jesus.

No matter what country you are from, if you are black you must answer to Jesus.

If you are white, the Commandments of Jesus are for you to keep.

If you are brown, the Commandments of Jesus are for you to keep.

If you are black, the Commandments of Jesus are for you to keep.

There are three major colors of people on this earth all around the world.

Even the majority of Asian people have white skin, as do the Jews.

There is no such thing as a yellow skin complexion — there are only white, brown and black people in this world.

No matter if you are white, Jesus is coming back again to take you to heaven if you are saved in Him.

No matter if you are brown, Jesus is coming back again to take you to heaven if you are saved in Him.

No matter if you are black, Jesus is coming back again to take you to heaven if you are saved in Him.

If you are white, you must confess and repent of your sins and live a renewed life unto Jesus.

If you are brown, you must confess and repent of your sins and live a renewed life unto Jesus.

If you are black, you must confess and repent of your sins and live a renewed life unto Jesus.

If you are white, you are a sinner saved through grace.

If you are brown, you are a sinner saved through grace.

If you are black, you are a sinner saved through grace.

No matter what country you are from, if you are white, you will be lost in your sins if you don't believe in Jesus Christ.

No matter what country you are from, if you are brown, you will be lost in your sins if you don't believe in Jesus Christ.

No matter what country you are from, if you are black, you will be lost in your sins if you don't believe in Jesus Christ.

Jesus lives with no sins to truly break the color barriers for all people white, brown and black to be equal in His holy eyesight that doesn't overlook anyone whether they are white, brown or black to be saved in Him before it is too late.

No One's

No one's thoughts can pass by the Lord.

No one's words can pass by the Lord.

No one's actions can pass by the Lord.

No one's dreams can pass by the Lord.

No one's disappointments can pass by the Lord.

No one's grief can pass by the Lord.

No one's misfortunes can pass by the Lord.

No one's heartaches can pass by the Lord.

No one's hatred can pass by the Lord.

No one's love can pass by the Lord.

No one's motives can pass by the Lord.

No one's intentions can pass by the Lord.

No one's feelings can pass by the Lord.

No one's mind can pass by the Lord.

No one's heart can pass by the Lord.

No one's sacrifice can pass by the Lord.

No one's intelligence can pass by the Lord.

No one's wisdom can pass by the Lord.

No one's knowledge can pass by the Lord.

No one's obedience can pass by the Lord.

No one's success can pass by the Lord.

No one's wealth can pass by the Lord.

No one's poverty can pass by the Lord.

No one's joy can pass by the Lord.

No one's sickness can pass by the Lord.

No one's plans can pass by the Lord.

No one's imagination can pass by the Lord.

No one's victory can pass by the Lord.

No one's defeat can pass by the Lord.

No one's biography can pass by the Lord.

No one's theories can pass by the Lord.

No one's educated guesses can pass by the Lord.

No one's education can pass by the Lord.

No one's strength can pass by the Lord.

No one's skills can pass by the Lord.

No one's talents can pass by the Lord.

No one's gifts can pass by the Lord.

No one's job can pass by the Lord.

No one's profession can pass by the Lord.

No one's fears can pass by the Lord.

No one's boldness can pass by the Lord.

No one's hope can pass by the Lord.

No one's religion can pass by the Lord.

No one's health can pass by the Lord.

No one's secrets can pass by the Lord.

No one's lies can pass by the Lord.

No one's evil deeds can pass by the Lord.

No one's good deeds can pass by the Lord.

No one's life can pass by the Lord.

No one's death can pass by the Lord.

No one's destiny can pass by the Lord.

No one's past can pass by the Lord.

No one's present can pass by the Lord.

No one's future can pass by the Lord.

No one's pride can pass by the Lord.

No one's mistakes can pass by the Lord.

No one's tears can pass by the Lord.

No one's desires can pass by the Lord.

No one's business can pass by the Lord.

No one's technology can pass by the Lord.

No one's science can pass by the Lord.

No one's novel can pass by the Lord.

No one's guilt can pass by the Lord.

No one's smile can pass by the Lord.

No one's laughter can pass by the Lord.

No one's jokes can pass by the Lord.

No one's disrespect can pass by the Lord.

No one's rudeness can pass by the Lord.

No one's favoritism can pass by the Lord.

No one's prejudices can pass by the Lord.

No one's injustice can pass by the Lord.

No one's pretense can pass by the Lord.

No one's deceit can pass by the Lord.

No one's magic can pass by the Lord.

No one's luck can pass by the Lord.

No one's hardships can pass by the Lord.

No one's doubts can pass by the Lord.

No one's comings and goings can pass by the Lord.

No one's material things can pass by the Lord.

No one's rules can pass by the Lord.

No one's laws can pass by the Lord.

No one's opinions can pass by the Lord.

No one's surprises can pass by the Lord.

No one's bad behavior can pass by the Lord.

No one's choices can pass by the Lord.

No one can pass by the Lord, who sees all things seen and unseen.

Nothing can pass by the Lord here on earth and throughout the universe.

Nothing in heaven can pass by the Lord God who is present to surround all existence forever and ever.

No angel in heaven and no fallen angel from heaven can pass by the Lord God who is everywhere at the same time.

The Lord God can pass by you and me who will not know it because of our sinful nature.

No one's documentary can pass by the Lord.

No one's age can pass by the Lord.

No one's ignorance can pass by the Lord.

No one's cries can pass by the Lord.

No one's selfishness can pass by the Lord.

No one's selflessness can pass by the Lord.

No one's rebellion can pass by the Lord.

No one's bondage can pass by the Lord.

No one's freedom can pass by the Lord.

No one's anger can pass by the Lord.

No one's unforgiveness can pass by the Lord.

No one's carelessness can pass by the Lord.

No one's will can pass by the Lord.

No one's tricks can pass by the Lord.

No one's high-minded ways can pass by the Lord.

No one's humility can pass by the Lord.

No one's charm can pass by the Lord.

No one's determination can pass by the Lord.

No one's innocence can pass by the Lord.

No one's righteousness can pass by the Lord.

No one's holiness can pass by the Lord.

No one's appearance can pass by the Lord.

No one's attitude can pass by the Lord.

No one's creation can pass by the Lord.

No one's authority can pass by the Lord.

No one's giving can pass by the Lord.

No one's sins can pass by the Lord.

Nothing can pass by the Lord God and exist, even for one second.

Nothing can pass by the Lord God and exist, even in a moment, in the blink of an eye.

No one's envy can pass by the Lord.

No one's jealousy can pass by the Lord.

No one's despair can pass by the Lord.

No one's faith can pass by the Lord.

No one's college degrees can pass by the Lord.

No one's assumptions can pass by the Lord.

No one's solutions can pass by the Lord.

No one's problems can pass by the Lord.

No one's confessions can pass by the Lord.

No one's repentance can pass by the Lord.

No one's culture can pass by the Lord.

No one's creed can pass by the Lord.

No one's race can pass by the Lord.

No one's color of skin can pass by the Lord.

No one's strife can pass by the Lord.

No one's truth can pass by the Lord.

No one's presence can pass by the Lord.

No one's existence can pass by the Lord.

No one's greed can pass by the Lord.

No one's status can pass by the Lord.

No one's stature can pass by the Lord.

No one's gender can pass by the Lord.

No one's gender fluidity can pass by the Lord.

No one can pass by the Lord God and live.

Lucifer couldn't pass by the Lord God when he was in heaven that God cast him out of with one third of the angels who had fallen from heaven.

No one's beauty can pass by the Lord.

No one's temperance can pass by the Lord.

No one's sufferings can pass by the Lord.

No one's gentleness can pass by the Lord.

No one's patience can pass by the Lord.

No one's accusations can pass by the Lord.

No one's heartlessness can pass by the Lord.

Nothing and no one can pass by the Lord God and still exist even for a moment.

No one's fame can pass by the Lord.

No one's greatness can pass by the Lord.

No one's superiority can pass by the Lord.

No one's peace can pass by the Lord.

No one's battle can pass by the Lord.

No one's war can pass by the Lord.

No one's world can pass by the Lord.

No one's delusions can pass by the Lord.

No one's illusions can pass by the Lord.

No one's circumstances can pass by the Lord.

Nothing can pass by the Lord God because everyone and everything would deteriorate before God would let anyone or anything pass Him and get the worship that is due to Him and His Son, Jesus Christ, who is eternal in oneness also with the Holy Spirit who no one can pass by and live to tell it.

No one's name can pass by the Lord who knows everyone's name, dead or alive.

No one can pass by the Lord who knew everyone's life before we were born.

No one can pass by the Lord who can make a genius look dumbfounded to His wisdom that He can give to simple people.

No one's experiences can pass by the Lord.

No one's foolishness can pass by the Lord.

No one's unfaithfulness can pass by the Lord.

No one's brokenness can pass by the Lord.

No one's wholeness can pass by the Lord.

No one's compassion can pass by the Lord.

No one's troubles can pass by the Lord.

No one's time can pass by the Lord.

No one's credit can pass by the Lord.

No one's politeness can pass by the Lord.

No one's clue can pass by the Lord.

No one's possessions can pass by the Lord.

No one's justice can pass by the Lord.

No one's judgment can pass by the Lord.

No one's discrimination can pass by the Lord.

No one's inequality can pass by the Lord.

No one's fears can pass by the Lord.

No one's destiny can pass by the Lord.

No one's aim can pass by the Lord.

No one's insecurity can pass by the Lord.

No one's trust can pass by the Lord.

No one's burden can pass by the Lord.

No one's depression can pass by the Lord.

No one's mental illness can pass by the Lord.

No one's stress can pass by the Lord.

No one's obstacles can pass by the Lord.

No one's trials can pass by the Lord.

No one's loyalty can pass by the Lord.

No one's meanness can pass by the Lord.

No one's vigor can pass by the Lord.

No one's excitement can pass by the Lord.

No one's boredom can pass by the Lord.

No one's whoredom can pass by the Lord.

No one's crimes can pass by the Lord.

No one can have anything pass by the Lord.

No one's honor can pass by the Lord.

No one's dignity can pass by the Lord.

Nothing can pass by the Lord God because we are nothing without the Lord and can believe that we are something special.

Nothing can pass by the Lord God, who created all things out of nothing.

Only the Lord can do this, not evolution which is like air pollution that can cause us to have a lung disease that will shorten our lives.

No one can pass by the Lord God, who hid Moses in the crevice of the rock and covered him with His hand.

God passed by Moses with all of His glory that Moses could not look upon and live to tell anyone.

The Lord God can pass by you and me who can't pass by God, even with our best efforts that will fall short of the glory of God.

No one's best foot forward can pass by the Lord God and achieve any recognition from God, who is worthy to be worshipped and praised forever and ever.

Like an Island Sitting All Alone

Our free will choice is like an island sitting all alone because God will not choose for us; we must make a choice all alone.

An island will sit all alone above the deep sea waters every day, just like you and I must make our choices all alone.

I have my mind and you have your mind to think on what choices to make.

I can choose what to say and you can choose what to say, even on the spur of the moment.

I can choose what to do and you can choose what to do, even on the spur of the moment.

God won't interfere with the choices we make all alone just like an island sitting all alone above the ocean waters.

An island will surely stand out all alone day after day that God won't make us choose to love and obey Him.

The devil can't make us choose to do evil on any day that our free will choices are like an island sitting all alone above the deep ocean waters.

No one can make anyone do anything against their free will choice, whether the choices are good choices or bad choices.

We choose to think what we want to think.

We choose to say what we want to say.

We choose to do what we want to do.

Nothing in this world is more free than our free will choices that are so all alone between God and the devil every day.

Our free will choice is like an island sitting all alone by itself while being surrounded by the deep waters, just like good and evil surrounds our free will choices that stand out and above everything in this world.

Our free will choice is like an island sitting all alone by itself.

Our destiny will greatly surround our free will choices every day that an island is sitting all alone above the deep ocean waters.

A Spiritual Closet

Everybody has a spiritual closet and only Jesus always knows what is inside it.

Every day we have a spiritual closet that we need to pray to Jesus to clean out because only Jesus can do that for you and me.

We can't clean out our spiritual closets that have some sins in them that we don't even know about because they are unseen to us.

We have seen sins and unseen sins in our spiritual closets that we need to open up and let Jesus come in and clean out.

We have closets in our houses that we can fill up with things to hold onto.

We have a spiritual closet where we need to get rid of the junk of our sins that Jesus sees when no one else can see them.

Our spiritual closets will hold us captive due to our secret sins if we don't confess and repent of them unto Jesus Christ.

A closet is a very closed-in place where we don't want to be because it will make us feel uncomfortable.

We know that a closet is not a good place to be in on any day.

We know that a closet will isolate us from going anywhere.

Our spiritual closet will isolate us from going anywhere with Jesus who wants to take us to spiritual heights in His holy word that is no secret closet for the world to not see the truth that will set us free from the devil's lies.

We can go into our spiritual closet and not even realize it until the Holy Spirit opens the door and pulls us out to see that only Jesus can cleanse us even from our secret sins.

A closet is nothing to cherish because no one likes being locked up in a closet.

We will lock ourselves up in our spiritual closets if we live in sin that throws away the key.

Only Jesus can find the key and unlock our spiritual closets and let us out with His mercy and grace to give us a second chance to deny ourselves and pick up our crosses and follow Him to where there are no spiritual secret closets to hold us captive in the darkness of sin.

We know that it can be dark in a closet and there's not much space to move around.

A spiritual closet is much worse because our secret sins will close its four walls very tight on us and suffocate us so we spiritually die.

Nobody in their right mind would want to be locked up in a closet, but many people cherish their spiritual closets filled with secret sins like they're the best thing that can happen to them because they enjoy living in their secret sins.

We create our own spiritual secret closets if we hold onto even one unconfessed sin that Jesus wants to save us from.

We must choose to let Jesus clean out our spiritual closets that will sooner or later pile up with the junk of sin.

In the Wilderness of Our Minds

The Lord can appear to us in the wilderness of our minds to protect our thoughts from the predators of temptations.

The Lord can comfort us in the wilderness of our minds where our thoughts can get uncomfortable because we're thinking on worldly things that can rust and erode.

The Lord can find us in the wilderness of our minds where we can be so lost for not staying in prayer and not reading God's holy word.

The Lord will lead us safely through the wilderness of our minds for thinking on Him and choosing to follow Him on our good days and bad days.

The Lord can quench our thirst in the wilderness of our minds for having faith in Him who will energize our minds with His encouragement for us to keep going on beyond the scorching heat of false doctrines that try to scorch our minds with the devil's lies.

The Lord can feed our minds with His spiritual food in the wilderness of our minds so that our minds are filled with pure and holy thoughts to satisfy our spiritual appetites.

We know that the wilderness is not a good place to go to because there is nothing good in the wilderness for us to see and hold onto.

We know that the wilderness is a hard place to live and we don't want to live there.

We know that the wilderness has nothing good to give us to survive on.

Jesus was in the wilderness for forty days and forty nights, and He was tempted by the devil who believed he had an advantage over Jesus in the wilderness.

Jesus prayed and fasted and spoke the word of God to the devil in the wilderness, and the devil failed to cause Jesus to sin against God in His mind.

The devil knew that if he could cause Jesus to think about eating the physical food it would break His fasting and the devil would get the victory over Jesus in the wilderness.

That was the first real test for Jesus, but He kept His mind on His Heavenly Father God and did not think about His appetite as the devil tried to tempt Him.

Jesus did not fail His great mission to save us from our sins.

We all have a wilderness in our minds that can think on the predators of sin.

We all can have thoughts of unaware sins that can prey on our minds if we don't stay prayed up to Jesus who the wilderness obeyed when Jesus was in the wilderness.

Even the wilderness knew that the devil didn't stand a chance when going up against Jesus.

Jesus created the wilderness experience for you and me so we can know what it means to trust and obey Him, even in the scorching heat and freezing cold wilderness of making Jesus our ultimate choice in our minds every day.

It's the Holy Spirit who gives us all the truth in the wilderness of our minds to satisfy our spiritually hungry souls.

It's the Holy Spirit who gives us all the truth in the wilderness of our minds to quench our spiritual thirst.

It's the Holy Spirit who gives us spiritual gifts in the wilderness of our minds to think on building up the church of Jesus Christ.

It was the Holy Spirit who strengthened Jesus to withstand all of the devil's temptations in the wilderness.

The wilderness of our minds is the greatest test for us to pass or fail in life's uncertainty, disappointments and shortcomings, because only Jesus can always improve our minds to lead our thoughts into a paradise of actions.

The wilderness of our minds is where we begin our ministry journey that will not always be easy for our minds to think on winning souls to Jesus Christ, especially when our enemies taunt us and make us think bad thoughts and maybe follow through on them.

The wilderness of our minds is where Jesus can walk through and find us so He can raise us up from being spiritually dead because God's goodness can surely lead us to repent in the wilderness of our minds.

Discover

God allows the astronomers to discover the things that His Son Jesus created in the outer space.

God allows the scientists to discover the creatures that His Son Jesus created down in the oceans.

Whatever anyone discovers, God allows it to be discovered because His Son Jesus created it.

Whatever the astronomers discover in the outer space, it's nothing new to Jesus.

Whatever scientists discover is nothing new to Jesus.

Jesus created all things and Jesus knows all things.

No one in this world will discover everything Jesus created in this world, and they surely won't discover everything He created in the outer space.

Jesus created these things for His glory and pleasure.

The most genius minds are limited to discover all the hidden things in this world where Jesus once lived without sin and knew every seen and unseen thing in this world because He created them.

No one can discover what God doesn't allow to be discovered.

Whatever God allows anyone to discover will surely let God-fearing people know that His Son Jesus is the creator of all things.

No astronomer and no scientist will ever discover all the things that Jesus created in the outer space and in this world.

Anyone can be sitting on a new discovery and not know it.

This comes to show that if God doesn't allow us to discover something, then it won't happen no matter how genius anyone might be.

Only Going Through the Motions

Are you only going through the motions of thinking about whatever you want to think about?

Are you only going through the motions of saying whatever you want to say?

Are you just going through the motions of going wherever you want to go?

Are you just going through the motions of wearing whatever you want to wear?

Are you just going through the motions of looking at whatever you want to look at?

Are you just going through the motions of picking up whatever you want to pick up?

Are you just going through the motions of eating whatever you want to eat?

Are you just going through the motions of drinking whatever you want to drink?

Are you just going through the motions of believing whatever you want to believe?

Are you just going through the motions of listening whatever you want to listen to?

Are you just going through the motions of doing whatever you want to do?

If you don't make Jesus Christ your purpose in life, then you will only go through the motions of existing in this life.

If you don't make Jesus Christ your hope in life, then you will only go through the motions of surviving in this life.

Only going through the motions is no real, strong foundation in anyone's life and it won't withstand the devil's evilness and wickedness.

Only going through the motions is no protection from the devil's schemes.

Only going through the motions is no Christian living unto the Lord Jesus Christ, who had a purpose and mission to save us from our sins.

Are you only going through the motions of being here in the land of the living with no heart to love and obey Jesus Christ, who gave us God's love, mercy, grace and truth so we would have a second chance to live our true purpose doing God's holy will?

The devil loves to give any one of us a joy ride in a limousine of only going through the motions, which will surely take us to the dead end of being lost in our sins.

Are you only going through the motions of reading whatever you want to read?

Are you only going through the motions of writing whatever you want to write?

Only going through the motions in life means a life destined for emptiness.

Only Jesus Christ can truly fill us with true purpose to glorify God who forever reigns over only going through the motions.

Who Can We Trust More than Jesus?

Who can we trust more than Jesus to make us well when we are sick?

Who can we trust more than Jesus to take away our pain?

Who can we trust more than Jesus to help us feel better?

Who can we trust more than Jesus to work out our problems?

Who can we trust more than Jesus to help us to move on in life?

Who can we trust more than Jesus to give us the right answer to our questions?

Who can we trust more than Jesus to strengthen us when we are weak?

Who can we trust more than Jesus to give us justice?

Who can we trust more than Jesus to lift us up when we are feeling down?

Who can we trust more than Jesus to understand us?

Who can we trust more than Jesus to stand by us?

Who can we trust more than Jesus to be real with us?

Who can we trust more than Jesus to love us?

Who can we trust more than Jesus to be our friend?

Who can we trust more than Jesus to tell us the truth?

Who can we trust more than Jesus to protect us?

Who can we trust more than Jesus to give us what we need?

Who can we trust more than Jesus to get us out of trouble?

Who can we trust more than Jesus to make things right for us?

Who can we trust more than Jesus to be patient with us?

Who can we trust more than Jesus to help us to be successful?

Who can we trust more than Jesus to help us to be well-balanced?

Who can we trust more than Jesus to help us to eat right?

Who can we trust more than Jesus to help us to think right?

Who can we trust more than Jesus to help us to talk right?

Who can we trust more than Jesus to help us to live right?

Who can we trust more than Jesus to help us to not make the same mistakes?

Who can we trust more than Jesus to help us to be wise?

Who can we trust more than Jesus to help us to make good choices in our lives?

Who can we trust more than Jesus to give us hope?

Who can we trust more than Jesus to forgive us?

Who can we trust more than Jesus to set the right example for us?

Who can we trust more than Jesus to support us?

Who can we trust more than Jesus to believe us?

Who can we trust more than Jesus to not change on us?

Who can we trust more than Jesus to talk to us?

Who can we trust more than Jesus to listen to us?

Who can we trust more than Jesus to be true to us?

Who can we trust more than Jesus to encourage us?

We can't trust anyone more than trusting Jesus.

We can't trust ourselves more than trusting Jesus.

We were born in sin to be in our genetics and we can't trust that.

Jesus lived in this world without sin in his flesh for us to put all of our trust in Jesus Christ.

We were born in sin to be in our flesh that we can't trust.

We can put all of our trust in Jesus who gave up His life on the cross and rose from the grave to save us from our sins.

Who can we trust more than Jesus?

What can we trust more than Jesus Christ, who we can trust to come back again and take us to heaven that is forever above everything in this world that will one day pass away with nothing to trust in.

Some Things are Best Left Behind in the Past

Some things are best left behind in the past and not talked about at all because that may cause someone to stumble or fall into disappointment.

Some things are best left behind in the past and not written about because that may cause someone to stumble or fall into discouragement.

Some things are best left behind in the past and not revealed because that may cause someone to stumble or fall into wanting revenge.

Some things are best left behind in the past and not brought back up because that may cause someone to stumble or fall into unforgiveness.

Some things are best left behind in the past and not gossiped about because that may cause someone to stumble or fall into sadness.

Some things are best left behind in the past and not joked about because that may cause someone to have animosity.

Some things are best left behind in the past and not broadcasted because that may cause someone to stumble or fall into hatred.

Some things are best left behind in the past and not think about because that may cause you and me to stumble or fall into not moving on.

If the Lord can wipe away past committed sins, then who are we to bring up the bad things that happened in the past?

If the Lord can forgive us our past committed sins, then who are we to not forgive anyone who did us wrong in the past?

Some things are best left behind in the past, not used as an excuse to judge those who especially knew what was right to do and didn't do it.

The Lord truly knows all who confessed and repented of their past sins that Jesus left behind when He rose from the grave.

Some things are best left behind in the past and everybody doesn't need to know them because it may cause someone to stumble or fall into holding onto their past mistakes that God had covered with His mercy and grave that brought us all this far to see this day when we all deserved to have died in the past.

We Trace Back to Our Original First Parents

Everyone's family tree will trace back to our original first parents, Adam and Eve, who we all truly come from.

Everybody in this world will trace back to our original first parents who God created and put them in the Garden of Eden.

The bible will take us back to our original first parents in the book of Genesis to show everybody in this world the root of our family tree.

We all will trace back to our original first parents, Adam and Eve, who populated this whole world with billions of human beings.

All around the world, everybody's blood is red and traces back to our original first parents, Adam and Eve.

All round the world everybody must drink water and eat food to live, which traces back to our original first parents, Adam and Eve.

Our family tree can go no further back than to our original first parents, Adam and Eve.

Our family tree cannot go outside of our original first parents, Adam and Eve.

There is no other family tree that anyone can claim beyond our original first parents, Adam and Eve, who everybody in this world came from because God made it to be that way.

We all have a spiritual family tree through our original Savior of the world to redeem everyone in the family of God.

Jesus is our spiritual parent, giving anyone a new spiritual birth for confessing and repenting of our sins unto Him and living our renewed lives unto Him.

We trace back to our original first parents, Adam and Eve, who are the root of everybody's family tree.

Every child of God can trace back to Jesus Christ, who predestined a spiritual family tree for every Christian who ever lived and is alive today to be in the family of God, whose family tree is destined for eternity with no demonizing exposures in God's family.

When it Comes to Winning Souls

When it comes to winning souls to the Lord, we believe that we are only supposed to reach out to the people who are not in the church.

We usually believe that the only lost souls are the people who don't go to church to worship the Lord and give Him all the glory and praise.

When it comes to winning souls to the Lord, it's for the people in the church too because there are people who go to church and are still of the world.

When it comes to winning souls to the Lord, it's also for the people in the church where there are people who are not saved in Jesus Christ, our Lord.

There are people in the church who are not of the church and you and I need to minister to them with our spiritual gifts from the Lord.

Everybody who goes to church doesn't believe in Jesus Christ, and they're only going through the motions of going to church with no true newness of life in Jesus Christ.

When it comes to winning souls to the Lord, we usually believe that just because there are people in the church then they must already be saved in Jesus from the pulpit to the church pews, but many souls are not rooted and grounded in Jesus Christ.

Winning souls is for church folks too because we need to give all of our minds, hearts, and souls to Jesus every day, not just one day out of the week that we usually go to church.

You and I will usually believe that the people who don't go to a church at all are the ones for us to win to the Lord.

There are people who have been going to church all of their lives but they are not converted and need to be won to the Lord.

Winning souls to the Lord is also for us church folks who need to deny self and pick up our crosses to follow Jesus, who we need to be like every day.

When We Fall Asleep

When we fall asleep, we are not aware of anything going on around us.

When we fall asleep, we don't see anything.

When we fall asleep, we don't feel anything.

When we fall asleep, we don't know anything, like we're dead.

When we fall asleep, it's like we're dead to the world.

Many people are spiritually asleep and aren't aware of the spiritual things of the Lord.

Many people are spiritually asleep and aren't aware of having faith in Jesus Christ.

Many people are spiritually asleep and aren't aware of praying to Jesus.

Many people are spiritually asleep and aren't aware of trusting Jesus.

Many people are spiritually asleep and aren't aware of calling on Jesus' holy name.

Many people are spiritually asleep and aren't aware of confessing and repenting of their sins unto Jesus.

Many people are spiritually asleep and aren't aware denying self and picking up one's cross to follow Jesus.

Many people are spiritually asleep and spiritually dead to the Lord Jesus Christ.

Jesus wakes us up in the morning out of our physical sleep so we can be conscious and aware of what is going on around us.

Jesus can wake up anyone out of their spiritual sleep for choosing to believe in Him who is forever alive beyond and above our conscious awareness and deep sleep.

When we fall asleep we are not even consciously aware enough to know if we are snoring in our sleep.

Many people are spiritually snoring out loud with the temporary things in their lives.

Jesus surely hears their snores in their spiritual sleep.

When we fall asleep, we have no conscious awareness of whether we will wake up again.

There are church folks who are falling asleep spiritually and they're spiritually snoring out loud about their desires for this sinful world.

Studying God's holy word and living by God's holy word will give anyone a spiritual awakening out of the spiritual sleep in this world.

One day, there will be a great spiritual awakening for all the world when Jesus comes back again on the clouds of glory for every eye to see Him, but that spiritual awakening will be too late for all who will fall dead at the brightness of Jesus' holy light.

The Lord's great spiritual awakening will be too much for the wicked to bear because they refused to believe in Jesus Christ to be saved.

www.ingramcontent.com/pod-product-compliance
Lightning Source LLC
Chambersburg PA
CBHW070914120626
46546CB00001B/256